THE EMOJI CODE

THE EM😂JI C😜DE

The Linguistics Behind
Smiley Faces and Scaredy Cats

Professor Vyvyan Evans

Picador | New York

picadorusa.com • picadorbookroom.tumblr.com
twitter.com/picadorusa • facebook.com/picadorusa

Picador® is a U.S. registered trademark and is used by Macmillan Publishing
Group, LLC, under license from Pan Books Limited.

For book club information, please visit facebook.com/picadorbookclub or
email marketing@picadorusa.com.

The Library of Congress Cataloging-in-Publication Data is
available upon request.

ISBN 978-1-250-12906-2 (hardcover)
ISBN 978-1-250-12907-9 (ebook)

Our books may be purchased in bulk for promotional, educational,
or business use. Please contact your local bookseller or the Macmillan Corporate
and Premium Sales Department at 1-800-221-7945, extension 5442,
or by email at MacmillanSpecialMarkets@macmillan.com.

Originally published in Great Britain by Michael O'Mara Books Limited

First U.S. Edition: August 2017

10 9 8 7 6 5 4 3 2 1

For Monica … the love of my life.

Once in a lifetime you meet
someone who changes everything!
True love's way began with Emoji.

CONTENTS

Prologue: Beginnings

Everything has a beginning. This story's was in January 2015. It was a Friday afternoon at the end of the month, and I was in the middle of completing a mortgage application. Keen for a distraction, I kept clicking over to my email. One such click revealed a message from a desk editor at the *Guardian* newspaper, in London, asking me to call. Curious to see what was up, I dialled her number.

It turned out that there was a news story breaking that no one seemed to know quite how to handle. An American teenager had just been arrested in New York for making an alleged terroristic threat against the police. But what had the journos in a tizz was this: the death threat had been made using nothing but emojis, the small colourful pictograms that, today, over 90 per cent of us use to pepper our interactions on our smartphones, and on social media. 'There aren't many language experts that even know what an emoji is. Can you write something that makes sense of this?' the desk editor asked. Intrigued, I set aside the mortgage documents. 'Let me think about it,' I replied. 'I need something this afternoon,' she countered, apologetically. 'Hmm … OK,' I said. And while I didn't know it at the time, with those few words, an entirely new research project that would run for years and a new linguistic science of text-based digital communication was born.

I spent the rest of the afternoon reflecting on the phenomenon of Emoji. I thought about the emojis I used, safe in my comfort zone, the boring ones: the wink, smile and, sometimes, a sad face. Before then, I'd never thought much about whether there were other emojis, or even where they came from. I tried to recall when I had first become aware of them. I struggled. One day they just seemed to be there, all at once, as if they had been dropped out of the sky and into our smartphones. Today emojis really do seem to be everywhere. But back in early 2015, people were just starting to use them in numbers. And I had to admit it, I didn't have a clue what some of them were supposed to convey. For instance, what did that one of the dancing twin girls with bunny ears mean?

As I began to investigate, I quickly discovered that emojis were a very recent phenomenon. It was only in 2011 that they were introduced as standard on the Apple electronic keyboard, on iPhones and iPads. They became available as standard with Windows 8 in 2012, but didn't receive full functionality across all internet browsers until Windows 10 in 2015. And on Android operating systems, which are used by the world's biggest-selling smartphone manufacturer, Samsung, they were not standard until 2013. But 2015 seemed to be the year that Emoji made the leap from some bizarre, little-known adolescent joke, to a bona fide means of communicating with our nearest and dearest, expressing something more than what could be achieved with digital text alone. By the end of 2015,

Emoji even received institutional respectability – of sorts – being endorsed by Oxford University Press: an emoji, no less, was named as Oxford Dictionaries' Word of the Year. Emoji could no longer be pigeon-holed as an amusing irrelevance, a passing fad; Emoji had gone mainstream!

I wrote my article, 'Can emojis be used to make terror threats?', and sent it through to the *Guardian*, which published it a few days later. And that was that. For the next couple of months I thought no more about it. I taught at the university, travelled to give international lectures, began work on a different book (and I completed my mortgage application, and moved house).

But the story resumed in April 2015. And this time, it wouldn't let me go. I was contacted by the London-based telecommunications company TalkTalk. Their mobile-phone division wanted to commission some research for a prospective PR campaign. They were interested in figuring out how widely Emoji was used by the UK's smartphone users, and, perhaps more importantly, how people use it, and why. Today reports on Emoji usage are everywhere; marketing companies, app developers and multinationals invest thousands and even millions in studying usage patterns. But in early 2015, little was known about these matters – TalkTalk confessed to having struggled to find an expert who could help them. My article from two months earlier had sent them my way. And so I helped design a questionnaire on usage patterns that was then used by a market research company, which polled 2,000 representative adults. I analysed the results, and in doing so, produced the world's first study into individual Emoji usage patterns. And from there, as the findings accumulated, the questions mushroomed in equal measure. The only solution to make sense of it all, I realised, was to set aside the book I was working on and write this one instead.

The rapid adoption of Emoji, in just a few years, makes it a rich (and well-recorded) case through which to explore the nature of human communication, including the nature and functions of language and other non-verbal aspects of communication. In the chapters that follow, I discuss a wide range of issues in the context of digital communication, and how these new communicative possibilities are changing the way we interact with our digital 'friends' and 'followers', many of whom we have never met. In our investigation into the world of Emoji, we'll explore the nature of communication, how grammar works, the evolutionary origins of language, the social and cultural factors that govern language use, language change and its development, as well as the nature and organisation of language, what it reveals about the nature of the human mind, and how meaning arises when we communicate. As we'll see, far from being some passing fad, Emoji reflects, and thereby reveals, fundamental elements of communication; and in turn, this all shines a light on what it means to be human. Surprising as it may sound for the uninitiated, there's far more to Emoji than you might think!

Now for an aside on terminology. The eagle-eyed will have noticed already that I sometimes spell Emoji with a capital first letter: E. When I do so, I am referring to Emoji as a set of glyphs, with rules, conventions and constraints, that is used as a system of communication. And when I use emoji without an initial capital, or when I refer, in the plural, to emojis, I have in mind the individual glyphs that populate the system.

But Emoji, while a system of communication, is a code, not a language, as reflected in the title of this book. Sometimes Emoji behaves in remarkably language-like ways; not surprising really, given that language is also a system designed, ultimately, to facilitate communication. But sometimes, quite often in fact, Emoji differs quite markedly from language, in its organisation and use. Emojis, for instance, are often repeated, adding emphasis by visual repetition. But what sane individual repeats the same English phrase over and over? A line of red hearts intuitively works, making the point clear. But *I love you*, the English expression, is more powerful when uttered or written just once. With undue repetition, it can come to seem insincere. Just as with the forced writing of lines by a punished schoolchild, the laborious begets boredom.

In this book, I explore the points of similarity between Emoji and language, as well as their differences. I also explore and contrast other systems of communication, including those that provide us with our full range of communicative resources.

While our focus is on Emoji, a recurring theme concerns the nature of the relationship between language and communication. Language is the world's most complex, naturally occurring behaviour. We all have a vested interest in it. By the age of four, every typically developing child on the planet is a linguistic genius – something beyond the ken of any other species. And language is something that varies dramatically across different human populations, in diverse and often startling ways.

We'll see that text-based digital communication – any non-spoken interaction between two or more people that is conducted using an electronic device, including but not limited to SMS, instant messaging and social media posts – reuses similar cognitive and interpersonal strategies to those that already exist. And specifically, Emoji, like other systems of communication, builds on an evolutionarily deep-seated, species-specific impulse to cooperate. Crucially, though, in our brave, new twenty-first-century world of textual digital communication, Emoji is further expanding the human potential to communicate. So, let's begin to see how.

1

Is Emoji the New Universal 'Language'?

Getting married is often regarded as one of life's most significant events. It can distil our hopes and dreams, and reframe our everyday life; through its ritual and celebration and the serious business of taking vows, we commit to sharing our life with another. A wedding can also mark the liminal passage from a more tranquil existence to the greater challenge of making and, for some, raising a family, and all the responsibilities and pressures that come with that. And, of course, most of us feel nervous ahead of the big day.

In April 2015, tennis star Andy Murray married his long-term girlfriend, Kim Sears. As is often the case with today's celebrities, he sent a pre-wedding message to his bride, friends and followers. In the context of early twenty-first-century social media technology, this took the form of a tweet on the morning of his wedding day (see Figure 1 in the picture section). In the message Murray expressed his hopes and expectations for the day, as well as hinting at the nerves he no doubt felt. But what really got tongues wagging was the fact that his tweet was made up of nothing but emojis.[1]

Andy Murray's tweet conveys, in pictorial form, the day's events, as Murray expected them to unfold: the early morning preparations, the emotions, the journey to and from the church, the post-wedding partying, the consummation of the marriage and, finally, exhausted sleep. But, despite the headlines that it provoked at the time, Andy Murray's Emoji tweet is not an isolated phenomenon. In February 2015, the Australian Minister for Foreign Affairs, Julie Bishop, an avid Emoji user, conducted the world's first political interview entirely in Emoji – the interview was conducted via iMessage and published on the Buzzfeed website. In one question, Ms Bishop was asked to provide her emoji characterisations of various world leaders. Intriguingly, she identified the then Australian prime minister Tony Abbott as the running man, while Russian president Vladimir Putin was characterised as the angry red face.[2]

Even an institution as august as the BBC is not immune. Each Friday, the Newsbeat page on the BBC website – associated with BBC Radio 1 and aimed at younger listeners – publishes the news in Emoji. Radio listeners are invited to guess what the headline means. See whether you can figure out which headline the Emoji 'sentence' in Figure 2, in the picture section, relates to.[3]

Nor is the literary canon exempt: Ken Hale, a visual designer with a passion for Emoji, has translated, among other classics, Lewis Carroll's *Alice in Wonderland*, a book of 27,500 or so words, into a pictorial narrative consisting of around 25,000 emojis.[4] Some example Emoji 'sentences' provided by the artist are given in Figure 3.

Of course, it's incredibly hard to read Emoji sentences. It's for this very reason that the Newsbeat Emoji headline quiz *is* a competition. Part of the satisfaction of reading the 'translations' of the sentences, and the humour that we derive, comes from nodding your head in tacit understanding once you've read the words. The translations enable us to make sense of how the emojis might add up to a meaningful Emoji 'sentence'. But just as with the emojified version of *Alice in Wonderland*, this all goes to show that Emoji just doesn't function in the same way as a language. As we will see in more detail later in the book, Emoji lacks a grammar – a system of rules that lets us combine the individual glyphs into more complex units of meaning. And it is precisely for this reason that we require a helping-hand to make sense of the Newsbeat and *Alice in Wonderland* examples.

Emoji is becoming ubiquitous. The New York Public Radio station WNYC introduced a subway service, using emojis, to advise passengers of the status of particular New York City (NYC) subway lines. As the WNYC website explained, 'We're trying to estimate agony on the NYC subway by monitoring time between trains and adding unhappy points for stations typically crowded at rush hour.'[5] You can find an example in Figure 5 in the picture section.

In response a leading online magazine has developed an emojified map of London's underground rail system, affectionately known to Londoners as the Tube. Those familiar with London's landmarks will instantly recognise stations such as Angel, Bank, Piccadilly Circus and so on (see Figure 6 in the picture section).

But is this all a gimmick, a passing fad? Could Emoji ever truly replace language in our digital communication? Or will it develop into a fully fledged language in its own right? And why is it that the younger generation are the most avid Emoji users? And beyond this, what about literacy and spelling standards – are they inevitable casualties of the rise of Emoji? In the final analysis, what does the uptake of Emoji mean for language, and for the future of human communication in the digital age? These are the very issues that I address in this book. And in the process, we'll examine what language is, and isn't, what role it plays in communication, and what the Emoji code reveals about these issues.

The rise and rise of Emoji

Emoji is an anglicised version of two Japanese words – *e*, 'picture', and *moji*, 'character'. And for those who might not be crystal clear on the subject, emojis are the colourful symbols – the winks, smileys, love hearts and so on – embedded as single character images, or glyphs, in our digital keyboards. Since 2011, when they first became widely available on mobile computing devices, they have taken the world by storm. At the ingredients level, an emoji is a glyph encoded in fonts, like other characters, for use in electronic communication. It's especially prevalent in digital messaging and social media. An emoji, or 'picture character', is a visual representation of a feeling, idea, entity, status or event. From a historical perspective, the first emojis were developed in the late 1990s in Japan for use in the world's first mobile-phone internet system, then under development by Japanese telecommunications company NTT DoCoMo. There were originally 176 emoji characters. This figure mushroomed during the 2000s, driven by competition in the Japanese mobile computing sector. In 2009, the California-based Unicode Consortium, which specifies the international standard for the representation of text across modern digital computing and communication platforms, sanctioned a little over 700 emojis. These were based, primarily, on usage in Japanese mobile computing. The Unicode-approved emojis became available to software developers by 2010. At the time of writing, there are 1,851 emoji Unicode characters available to software developers, including skin-tone modifiers and various other combinations, sequences that produce couple and family emojis; but this figure will continue to rise[6] – for the most up-to-date information, the ultimate source of Emoji facts, figures and cross-platform glyphs is emojipedia.org.[7] But let's be clear from the outset: Emoji is not a language in the way that, say, English, French or Japanese are languages; at least not yet. I'll consider what makes something a language in Chapter 3, and how language-like Emoji is (and isn't). And I'll have a lot more to say on whether Emoji is likely to evolve into a language. That said, we need to be equally clear that Emoji represents a powerful system of communication; while not a language, it nevertheless fulfils some of the functions associated with language.

With that caveat in mind, the following fact is especially

discombobulating: Emoji is, today, incontrovertibly the world's first truly universal form of communication. Given that English is often said to be the world's global language, to make the point clear, a comparison with English is a highly instructive point of departure.

While English doesn't have the same number of first-language users as other languages – both Mandarin (900 million) and Spanish (427 million) have more native speakers – it has both status and reach that puts it on a different plane to any other. English has 339 million native speakers, with a further 603 million speakers who use it as a second language. This means there are around 942 million more-or-less fluent speakers in the world. And with another 500-plus million users with some degree of fluency, that makes for more than 1.5 billion people alive today with proficiency in English. It's the primary or official language in 101 countries, from Canada to Cameroon, and Malta to Malawi – far outstripping any other language.[8] It has been transplanted a great distance from its point of origin – a small country on a small island – spreading far beyond English shores. This was first achieved by the expansion and might of the British Empire, which at its height was the largest empire in history and the world's foremost economic power for well over a century. By 1913, around 412 million people, almost a quarter of the world's population at the time, were directly governed from London;[9] and following the Great War of 1914–18, the British Empire controlled territories amounting to 13,700,000 square miles, around a quarter of the world's total landmass.[10] Since the Second World War, with the United States superseding the United Kingdom as the world's most economically powerful nation, the influence of English has continued apace.

One interesting source of evidence of English's far-reaching, and at times curious, impact comes from pseudo-English – foreign words that sound somewhat strangely English but aren't. The Dutch and Germans refer to a mobile (or cell) phone as a 'handy', and many are even convinced this is an English term for this device. In Japan, the term is 'cellar phone'. More bizarrely, in France, a glamorous Parisienne might indulge in an 'unbrushing' – a hairstyling event in which one's hair is, counter-intuitively, styled (rather than unbrushed). In Moscow, the pseudo-Anglicism 'feyskontrol' (from *face control*) refers to the act of refusing entry at high-end nightclubs to those who aren't quite the type of beautiful people the nightclub desires. The list goes on. Today, the ubiquitous influence of English in a wide array of global communication contexts is staggering: from commerce to diplomacy, from aviation to academic publishing, English serves as the global lingua franca.

But here comes the undiplomatic put-down; in comparison, Emoji dwarfs even the reach of English.

There are several ways in which we can measure the stratospheric rise of Emoji. One is the rapid rate of smartphone adoption – a 'smart' phone being defined as a wireless phone with mobile internet capability, just to be crystal clear. Smartphones were among the earliest devices that deployed the electronic keyboards which featured emojis as standard. Today nearly one quarter of the global population owns a smartphone; based on a survey of mobile computing habits in forty-one countries, it is estimated that there are currently over 2 billion smartphones in the world, with the figure set to continue to rise.[11] By 2016, 3.2 billion people (approaching half the world's population) had regular internet access, and

75 per cent of internet users accessed the internet via smartphones.[12]

Looking at specific countries, China exceeded 500 million smartphones during 2014, and India achieved more than 200 million smartphone users by 2016; in the USA the same figure was achieved by 2017, by which point 65 per cent of the population of the United States owned a smartphone.[13] In terms of smartphones alone, by 2015 some 41.5 billion text messages were being sent globally every day; and across social media applications, each day more than 6 billion emojis are exchanged – mind-boggling figures.[14] The table opposite shows the smartphone rate of adoption for the twenty-five nations that are the most avid users.

Another measure for assessing the uptake of Emoji comes from its penetration in social media applications. Let's consider Instagram, the popular photo and video sharing platform. Instagram, founded in 2010, has well over 300 million active monthly users and counting, sharing over 70 million photos and videos every day.[16] In fact, by the end of 2014, one fifth of the world's internet users aged between sixteen and sixty-four had an Instagram account.[17] In the first month following the launch of the Emoji keyboard in iOS, the uptake of emojis in text and captions on Instagram photos jumped from zero to 10 per cent. This further accelerated with the incorporation of Emoji in Android platforms. And by March 2015, nearly half of all text on Instagram posts contained emojis. The graph below illustrates the trend.

Top 25 Countries, Ranked by Smartphone Users, 2015 - 2020

millions

	2015	2016	2017	2018	2019	2020
1. China*	512.6	552.2	593.4	643.6	690.9	732.5
2. India	184.0	223.6	267.1	305.9	347.5	381.5
3. US**	190.5	207.2	219.8	229.2	236.8	241.5
4. Indonesia	55.4	65.2	74.9	83.5	92.0	99.7
5. Brazil	55.4	63.9	71.7	78.9	84.5	89.1
6. Russia	53.8	60.2	66.5	70.6	73.3	75.2
7. Japan	51.8	55.8	58.9	60.9	62.6	64.2
8. Mexico	43.7	52.8	59.8	64.6	68.0	69.9
9. Germany	42.3	46.9	50.8	53.5	54.7	55.8
10. UK**	38.0	41.0	43.6	45.3	46.7	47.9
11. Vietnam	27.2	36.5	43.7	49.5	54.5	58.4
12. France	31.2	35.0	38.1	40.2	41.8	43.2
13. South Korea	33.6	34.6	35.6	36.5	37.0	37.5
14. Turkey	28.7	33.8	38.3	41.3	43.8	45.7
15. Italy	28.1	30.9	32.9	34.8	35.4	35.9
16. Spain	26.0	28.8	31.4	33.3	34.8	35.7
17. Philippines	24.6	28.6	31.8	34.9	37.4	39.9
18. Thailand	23.7	27.4	30.0	32.1	33.9	35.1
19. Canada	20.4	22.3	23.8	24.8	25.6	26.2
20. Egypt	18.2	21.0	23.6	25.8	27.9	30.1
21. Colombia	16.9	19.0	20.9	22.7	24.4	26.0
22. South Africa	14.9	17.9	20.7	23.0	24.9	26.9
23. Taiwan	16.4	17.2	17.8	18.3	18.6	18.8
25. Nigeria	14.5	17.0	19.7	22.5	25.5	28.6
25. Poland	14.6	16.8	19.0	20.4	21.4	22.2
Worldwide	1,893.4	2,133.8	2,354.9	2,556.4	2,738.9	2,895.4

Source: eMarketer, Sep 2016.[15] **Methodology:** estimates are based on the analysis of survey and traffic data from research firms and regulatory agencies, historical trends, and country-specific demographic and socioeconomic factors. **Note:** individuals of any age who own at least one smartphone and use the smartphone(s) at least once per month; *excludes Hong Kong; **forecast from Aug 2016. Smartphones are any voice handset with an advanced operating system (e.g. Android, BlackBerry, iOS, Windows Phone, etc.) and features/capabilities that resemble a PC.

Smartphone adoption rates.[15]

Yet another line of evidence, pointing to the rise and rise of Emoji, comes from the demise of textual forms of internet slang. For example, abbreviations used in SMS messages and social media applications, such as 'lol' (laugh out loud), 'lolz' (laugh out loud – with sarcasm), 'imao' (in my arrogant opinion – used to confidently assert something), or 'omg' (oh my god – used to express negative shock or surprise) are increasingly being replaced by the corresponding emojis.

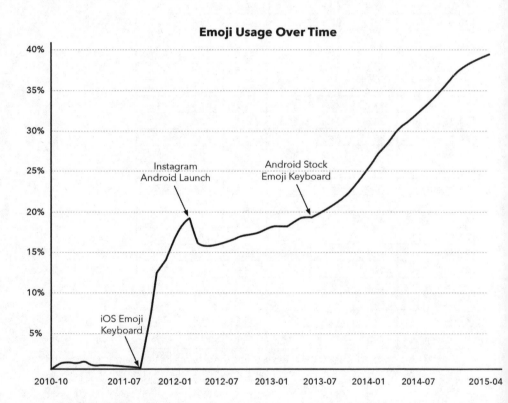

Emoji usage in Instagram captions.[18]

For instance, in text captions on Instagram, the smiley face has come to replace a range of internet abbreviations that have semantically related meanings. These include: lolol, lmao, lololol, lolz, lmfao, lmaoo, lolololol, lol, ahahah, ahahha, loll, ahaha, ahah, lmfaoo, ahha, lmaooo, lolll, lollll, ahahaha, ahhaha, lml, lmfaooo. Moreover, and unlike the slang terms, many of which are language-specific (as in they are different in English, German, Japanese etc.), Emoji is now a near-universal form of communication, across all language groups of Instagram users. The general pattern of internet slang being replaced by emojis is captured by the table below.

Comments	Internet Slang	Emojis
That's funny	haha/lol	😂
Okay	K	👌
I like it	like	👍
Talk to you later	ttyl	👋
Just kidding	jk	😉
I love you	ily	🖤

Emoji replacement of Internet slang.[19]

In the UK, research that I conducted demonstrates that around 80 per cent of adult smartphone users – defined as eighteen to sixty-five-year-olds – regularly use emojis in their text messages, with around 40 per cent of Brits having sent text messages, paradoxically, without text, containing emojis alone.[20] Beyond this, the live Twitter emojitracker, designed and curated by Brooklyn-based self-dubbed artist and hacker Matthew Rothenberg, reveals the numbers and types of emojis that are trending at any given time. Since the inauguration of emojitracker.com on 4 July 2013, Rothenberg has tracked over 16 billion tweets containing emojis – for the stats nerd, that's hundreds of tweets containing emojis every second of every day!

Ultimately, whatever the metric, the adoption rate of Emoji is staggering; and this provides grist to the mill that Emoji is a truly global form of communication. It matters not a jot whether your mother tongue is English, Finnish or Korean: the smiley face means the same thing in every language – we are all, or nearly all, 'speaking' Emoji now.

Bringing emojis to life

A common question that people ask is whether anyone can simply create their own emojis. The short answer is yes. For instance, Finland's Ministry of Foreign Affairs has created its own set of national emojis that express Finnish identity. These include emojis of people in saunas, of a Nokia phone and of a headbanger (see Figure 4 in the picture section).

But while Finland was the first country in the world to embrace its national identity through emojis, you won't find these pictograms on your smartphone digital keyboard any time soon. And that's because the Finnish emojis have not been officially sanctioned by the Unicode

Consortium – and Finland has no plans to submit them for consideration.

A new emoji (as opposed to a bespoke emoji created for a specific purpose, such as a tourism or marketing campaign) has to meet various criteria in order to begin its first, tentative steps in the rigorous vetting process that determines which emojis become officially sanctioned and thus subsequently appear on your smartphone digital keyboard. Indeed, the process can be lengthy, taking around eighteen months from an emoji achieving initial official 'candidate' status to becoming approved – and many emoji proposals are rejected out of hand, never even making it to the candidate stage. Even then, once an emoji passes muster and is approved, it can take still longer for the newly sanctioned emoji to make it onto our digital keyboards; emojis can take several operating system updates, and sometimes several years, to make it onto a smartphone or tablet computer near you. Accordingly, bespoke emojis, as in the case of the Finnish examples, are often referred to as 'stickers', rather than emojis. A sticker is a bespoke emoji-like image that has to be downloaded as part of an app from an online app store in order to be used in text messages or on social media.

On 25 January 2016, a Chinese-American businesswoman, Yiying Lu, from San Francisco, succeeded where Finland had declined to tread. Supported by a crowdfunding campaign, Lu was successful in having a dumpling achieve official emoji candidate status (see Figure 7 in the picture section). The idea was that the dumpling should be allowed to join a growing catalogue of food emojis, including pizza, hamburgers, doughnuts and even a taco, itself supported by a Change.org petition organised by Taco Bell – who else?

The entire emoji vetting process is controlled by a handful of American multinational corporations that make up Unicode. There are strict qualifying criteria for new emojis: for instance, they may not depict persons living or dead, nor deities. This is why there are no Buddha, John Lennon or Madonna emojis. In addition, for a proposed emoji to be accepted as a 'candidate' emoji – rather than being rejected out of hand, without further consideration – it must be deemed to have widespread appeal. On this score, the proposal for a dumpling emoji looks to be strong. A dumpling – at its most basic, a dough-wrapped food parcel – is popular around the world, with exemplars ranging from Italian ravioli to Russian *pelmeni*, to Japanese *gyoza*. In Argentina there are empanadas, Jewish cuisine has kreplach, in Korea there is *madoo* and China has potstickers. But when Lu, an aficionado of Chinese dumplings, attempted to text a friend about the dish, she noticed there wasn't an emoji she could use.

In early 2016, the fact that the dumpling had officially achieved candidate emoji status in California hit the headlines around the world; even the broadcast media got in on the act. I was invited onto BBC Radio to discuss the success of the Dumpling Project, headlining with Lu herself. The crowdfunded Kickstarter campaign had been a self-evident success, achieving over $12,000 and reaching its target within a few hours of going live. But the headlines begged the question: why all the fuss about dumplings? Isn't this simply frivolity gone mad, an expensive bit of silliness?

On the contrary: Emoji matters. The Dumpling Project stands for far more than a simplistic bid to have the favourite food of a Bay area businesswoman sanctioned as an emoji. It is an instance of internet democracy at work; indeed, the slogan of the project read: 'Emoji for the people, by the people'.

One significant reason why Emoji matters is the following: love it or loathe it, Emoji is, today, the world's global form of communication; as we've already seen, over 90 per cent of the world's internet users make use of emojis on social media applications,[21] and over 80 per cent of all adults regularly use emojis in smartphone text messages, with figures likely to be far higher for under-eighteens. In short, most of the world's mobile computing users use Emoji much of the time. And yet, the catalogue of emojis that show up on our smartphones and tablet computers – the vocabulary that connects around 2 billion people – is controlled by a handful of American multinationals. Eight of the eleven full members of the Unicode Consortium are American: Oracle, IBM, Microsoft, Adobe, Apple, Google, Facebook and Yahoo. In addition, the committee reps of these tech companies are overwhelmingly white, male, and computer engineers – hardly representative of the diversity exhibited by the global users of emojis (a point to which I will return later in the book). Indeed, as of 2015, the majority of food emojis were associated with North American culture, with some throwbacks to the Japanese origins of Emoji (such as a sushi emoji).

Hence, one motivation for the Dumpling Project was to ensure better representation. Of course, on its own, a campaign and proposal for a new food emoji cannot do much. But as an appeal to global cultural (and culinary) diversity, and as a clarion call for better representation of this diversity, the dumpling is a powerful emblem. Emoji began as a somewhat bizarre, little-known North Asian phenomenon; but since then, control has come to rest in the hands of American corporate giants. Dumplings, on the other hand, in their various shapes and guises are truly international; this speaks to the global nature of Emoji, as a form of quasi-universal communication fit for the digital age.

Another interesting aspect of the Dumpling Project is that it highlights the Byzantine process of emoji selection. Candidate status requires preparation of a detailed proposal, together with drawings of what the proposed emojis would look like; hence the need for funds from a Kickstarter campaign. The proposal is judged by a technical subcommittee of the Unicode Consortium before consideration by the full committee. This contrasts with the way in which a natural language such as English grows. For instance, anyone can coin a new word. But a newly minted word sinks or swims depending on whether it is useful for us, or otherwise valuable in some way. For instance, the term *computer mouse* – an invention first patented in 1970 and so-named because it physically resembles a small rodent – now relates to an invention that, for several decades, became a central and indispensable element of home computing. And the consequence is that the uptake of the word was driven, in this case, by real-world necessity rather than, as in the case of Emoji, a committee that rules on what is and is not permissible. It's worth noting that the plural for a computer mouse is not *mice*, which proves that *computer mouse* is a new word coinage, distinct from its rodent visual namesake. Indeed, and as we shall see later in the book, in the case of language academies, their attempts to maintain linguistic standards, keeping language pure amid malign external influences, typically fail; the French continue to blithely use the borrowed English 'email' and 'weekend', rather than the more verbose French equivalents (*courrier électronique; fin de semaine*), in spite of the hand-wringing of L'Académie française. Natural language is a living, evolving organism shaped and renewed each day by its users; consequently, language-oversight academies fail, where Unicode, with Emoji, succeeds.

In employing the dumpling as a conceit, Lu's project successfully engaged with, and educated, the public: both through the Kickstarter campaign, and the associated media publicity. One goal was to make the emoji-using public aware of the controls and tortuous process involved in new emojis seeing the light of day. Another was to demonstrate that, in principle, anyone can propose a new emoji that successfully navigates the time-consuming selection process. While there are caveats of course, as I discuss later on, every single one of us has the right to propose an emoji; and we don't have to be an erudite academic, elected to an arcane academy, donning odd-looking robes, to do so.

Perhaps more than anything, the Dumpling Project is fun; and in terms of Emoji, a sense of fun is the watchword. While these colourful glyphs add a dollop of personality to our digital messaging, the Dumpling Project makes a powerful and important point. It avoids gender, religion or politics in conveying a simple message about inclusiveness in the world's most widely used form of communication. And in the process, it provides us with an object lesson in the unifying and non-threatening nature of Emoji. Perhaps the world can, indeed, be united for the better by this new, quasi-universal form of communication.

Sex, communication
and emotional intelligence

Setting aside dumplings, there are serious questions here about why and how Emoji has come to be a truly global system of communication. Some see Emoji as little more than an adolescent grunt, taking us back to the dark ages of illiteracy. But as we shall see, this prejudice fundamentally misunderstands the nature of communication. And in so doing it radically underestimates the potentially powerful and beneficial role of Emoji in the digital age as a communication and educational tool.

All too often we think of language as the key player, the kingpin, in our everyday world of meaning.[22] But, in actual fact, much of the meaning we convey and glean in our everyday social encounters comes from non-verbal cues. In the spoken medium, gesture, facial expression, body language and speech intonation provide a means of qualifying and adjusting the message conveyed by the words we utter. A wink or smile nuances the language, providing a crucial cue, aiding our understanding of the spoken word. And intonation not only 'punctuates' our spoken language – there are no white spaces and full stops in speech that help us identify where words begin and sentences end – it also provides 'missing' information not otherwise conveyed by the words. We'll explore this further in Chapter 4.

Digital communication provides us with an important channel of communication in our increasingly connected social and professional lives. But the rich, communicative context available in face-to-face encounters is largely absent. Digital text alone is impoverished and, on occasion, emotionally arid. Textspeak – the messages and posts we produce using text, and which are transmitted electronically via messaging and social media applications – seemingly possesses the power to strip all forms of nuanced expression from even the best of us. But here Emoji can help: as we will see, it fulfils a similar function in digital communication to gesture, body language and intonation in spoken interaction. Emoji, in SMS text messaging, email and other forms of digital communication, enables us to better express tone and provide emotional cues, and this allows us to better manage the ongoing flow of information, and to interpret what the words are meant to convey.

In fact, the idea that digital text, used alone, sucks away the nuancing has even been given its own name: Poe's law. Based on comments made originally by Nathan Poe on how to parody fundamentalist views, Poe's law is now an internet adage, widely cited on web forums and chat rooms; it even has its own Wikipedia page.[23] According to British newspaper the *Daily Telegraph*, Poe's law states the following: 'Without a winking smiley or other blatant display of humour, it is impossible to create a parody of fundamentalism that someone won't mistake for the real thing.'[24] In other words, when poking fun in digital communication, emojis are best used for avoidance of doubt; nothing yells 'I'm being sarcastic, duh' like the rolling eyes emoji.

It is no fluke, therefore, that I have found that 72 per cent of British eighteen to twenty-five-year-olds believe that Emoji makes them better at expressing their feelings.[25] Far from leading to a drop in standards, Emoji is enabling people – especially the young – to become better communicators in their digital lives; the advent of Emoji can be seen, from this perspective, as empowering, a force for good in twenty-first-century communication.

A case in point can be found in research commissioned by the dating site Match.com in the United States. In the fifth annual *Singles in America* report, researchers investigated the relationship between Emoji usage and sexual conquests – the first survey of its kind to do so.[26] The survey polled over 5,600 singles – all non-Match.com subscribers – whose socio-economic and ethnic profiles were representative of the national population. And the results were striking: the more emojis a singleton uses in their digital communication, the more dates they get to go on; further, the more sex they have. A striking 54 per cent of those who report that they regularly use Emoji had sex, compared with 31 per cent of those that don't. Even more striking: for women, Emoji usage correlates with reported sexual satisfaction. The finding was that female singletons who use kiss-themed emojis reported having more orgasms than other women.

Clearly, and as any scientist worth their salt will warn us, correlation doesn't entail causation. You can't simply start using Emoji in your text messaging and expect to start being invited out on more dates (if only!) and certainly not that you'll magically have more orgasms. Rather, Emoji usage is indicative of something else. Using Emoji makes it easier for your potential date to gauge your message: Emoji facilitates a better calibration and expression of our emotions in digital communication. Biological anthropologist Helen Fisher of Rutgers University, and Chief Scientific Advisor to Match.com's annual *Singles in America* survey, commented on these findings: 'Here we have a new technology that absolutely jeopardizes your ability to express your emotion … there is no more subtle inflection of the voice … and so we have created another way to express emotions and that is the emoji.'[27]

In essence, it is not Emoji usage per se that gets you more dates; rather, Emoji users are more effective communicators – a point I will repeat throughout the book. Their messages have more personality, and better convey the emotional intent of the text message. In turn, this leads to greater emotional resonance in the recipient.

In general terms, the predominant global usage of Emoji does relate to emotions. In a survey conducted by London-based software developer SwiftKey, over 1 billion items of text-based data were analysed from users spread across sixteen different languages.[28] Interestingly, the top three Emoji categories all directly related to emotional expression. Happy faces, which include winks, kisses, smiles and grins, accounted for 45 per cent of all Emoji usage. Sad faces (including angry faces) made up 14 per cent of all usage. Heart emojis – of all colours, including the broken heart emoji – made up 12.5 per cent of usage. Over 70 per cent of emoji usage directly relates to emotional expression of some kind. This finding resonates with my own research that shows Emoji to be a powerful means of expressing emotion, which, users report, enables them to better connect with others in digital communication.

Today, the average adult in the United Kingdom – one example of a modern, digitally well-connected society – spends more than twenty hours per week online, with the under-twenty-four age group spending more than twenty-seven hours per week online.[29] Britons are also increasingly online while on the move, using smartphones to stay connected. In this era of 24/7 digital communication, textspeak is beginning to catch up with the repertoire of communicative tools we have in the spoken medium. Emoji is an empowering addition to the hitherto primarily textual format in the digital arena. As the nature and practice of using Emoji continues to develop and evolve, its significance will, it's safe to say, become less contested. In many ways, this is only the beginning.

2

Emoji Crime and the Nature of Communication

On 4 January 2015, at 12.55 p.m., Asiris Oristy posted a fateful Facebook update. The seventeen-year-old from Brooklyn, New York, was clearly frustrated, perhaps even angry. Being a young African-American, he would have no doubt felt a sense of outrage and poignant injustice at the spate of high-profile killings of young black men by white police officers. Oristy's bitterness seeped through in a series of posts where he assumed the perspective of white, trigger-happy officers, only too ready to shoot first and ask questions later. Examples include posts such as 'feel like katxhin a body right now', and 'Nigga run up on me, he gunna get blown down', posted on 15 January. Being black and running, so the derision seemed to imply, is, alas, probable cause in the so-called land of the free.

But it wasn't these sentiments that got Aristy into hot water. What really did it was his use of Emoji: four emojis, to be precise. On 4 January, Aristy posted a police officer emoji, followed by three handgun emojis pointing at it. He'd go on to repeat the sequence in further posts over the next few days. To make matters worse, his outraged posts were public: anyone on Facebook could read them.[30]

On 18 January, the New York Police Department obtained a warrant, arrested Oristy and, according to his lawyer, ransacked his home. Oristy was charged, under statutes introduced following 9/11, with making a terroristic threat – of threatening to kill members of the NYPD. The criminal complaint against Oristy alleged that, 'As a result of this conduct, the defendant has caused informant and other New York City police officers to fear for their safety, for public safety, and to suffer alarm and annoyance.'[31]

The basis for the charge was the four emojis, posted on Facebook, amounting to the world's very first alleged emoji terrorist offence. Like it or not, Emoji does matter. Emojis really are more than a mere inconsequential flourish to our digital talk. They represent a powerful communicative device that can even get you arrested.

This case throws up a number of fascinating questions surrounding the nature of human communication. Self-evidently, we don't need language to communicate; the case of Aristy and his Emoji post confirms this. And any schoolteacher will tell you that a smirk or snigger from a misbehaving schoolchild speaks volumes. So, what is the nature of communication? And what light does emoji crime shed on it?

The Conduit Metaphor

An everyday myth about communication is that meaning is akin to a physical object: something that can be, almost literally, packaged up into words. And in order to understand what someone means when they talk or write, we have to unpack their words, revealing the symbolic residue contained inside them, much as we might unwrap a birthday gift to reveal the surprise within. Perhaps more tellingly, even the way in which we talk, informally, about communication confirms this commonplace myth. We speak of *getting our ideas across, putting our thoughts into words,* of *a loaded word* or *expression,* of *dense prose* that is *impenetrable* or *unclear,* of a narrative being *pregnant with meaning.* We talk of friends, colleagues or lovers *giving us too much information,* or of *not giving us clear information.* We complain that our friends' ideas or feelings only *came through vaguely, unclearly,* or that we *couldn't find any meaning in there.*

But think about it for a second. Seeing communication in this way amounts to a metaphor – sure, we can put a birthday gift in a box, wrap it in glittery paper, and give it to someone; but we don't literally place our meanings into words, which are then unpacked, revealing the meaning within. As the influential metaphor analysts George Lakoff and Mark Johnson have pointed out, the commonplace way of thinking about communication involves this metaphor of language as a conduit.[32] It's as if ideas are solid things, with hard edges, that can be passed from one mind to another through the physical conduit of language.

According to this Conduit Metaphor, 'The speaker puts ideas (objects) into words (containers) and sends them (along a conduit) to a hearer who takes the idea/objects out of the word/containers.'[33] 'Getting' the meaning inlaid in the linguistic conduit involves a metaphorical process of unpacking the words. If we are confused, meaning is seen as having been lost in transmission. We say: *I couldn't decipher what she was saying*, or *His prose was too dense*. If someone doesn't get the point, we say: *She failed to unpack the argument*. If someone misunderstands or over-interprets, we say: *He took way too much from what I was saying*.

In classic research from 1979, the philosopher of language Michael Reddy has demonstrated that the Conduit Metaphor for communication has four main components, which we all buy into, whether we are aware of it or not.[34] Firstly, language serves as a conduit – a channel – through which ideas – meanings – travel from one person to another. Secondly, when we write or speak we are, essentially, inserting ideas into words and phrases. Thirdly, the transmission of meaning is achieved by the words being sent from one person to another. And finally, understanding is achieved when, upon reading or listening to someone else, we extract meaning from the words that have been sent through to us. In short, our commonplace view of communication is this: meaning is a thing that can be packaged up into words, and transmitted from one mind to another, through language.

If the Conduit Metaphor were merely an intuitive form of shorthand, allowing us to speak loosely about how communication works, all would be well. But alas, that is not the case: communication just doesn't work in the way the Conduit Metaphor would have us believe.

The shape-shifting malleability of meaning

For one thing, meaning is not something that is stable, that can be bundled up and transmitted via a language-conduit. And this is because the meaning associated with words, or indeed emojis, is not fixed; on the contrary, it varies.

Before getting to Emoji, let's take language first. On the face of it, to claim that meaning is a shape-shifter, that our words have the consistency of putty, changing shape – and meaning – may sound counter intuitive. But by this I am most definitely not saying that words have no meaning at all, that anything goes. In Lewis Carroll's children's classic *Alice Through the Looking Glass*, Carroll's language analyst-in-chief is Humpty Dumpty. And Humpty's cavalier approach is to deny any fixed meaning to a word: 'When I use a word,' Humpty Dumpty says, in rather a scornful tone, 'it means just what I choose it to mean – neither more nor less.' Of course, if Humpty were right, that a word can mean whatever he chooses, then language would abjectly fail to have any role whatsoever in communication, as we would each talk past or through one another: language would provide no semantic basis for any common ground.

But words must, self-evidently have, a relatively consistent, widely known meaning if they are to function effectively in spoken and written communication. After all, the difference in the meaning of this sentence: *She ran up the stairs*, compared to this one: *She ran down the stairs*, derives from the meaning that you and I attribute to *up* versus *down*. Both have relatively stable, commonly known meanings that relate to a difference in direction along the vertical axis – this is what it means to be speakers of a shared language.

But while linguistic meaning is a far cry from the 'anything goes' view of Humpty Dumpty, words are, indeed, malleable in what they can and do mean. An important reason for this is that we are forever interpreting what others are saying through the prism of the contexts in which words are embedded; what a word means is as much influenced by who says it, when they said it, and where, as by the face-semantic-value of the words themselves.

Take a famous example used by the language scientist Stephen C. Levinson. Levinson asks us to imagine hooking a bobbing bottle out of the sea. Upon releasing the cork, inside you find a piece of paper, with scrawled handwriting. The message reads: 'Meet me here a week from now with a stick about this big.'[35] Without knowing who wrote the message, the kind of gesture they were making, and where or when the note was written, we are at a loss to know what size stick we should bring, where we should bring it, on what date and time, nor even how to recognise the person we should deliver it to. So, without the necessary context, we are at a loss to know what is required of us.

Setting aside castaways and messages in a bottle, here's a real-life and altogether more down-to-earth example. You are waiting in a queue in a fast-food restaurant. As your turn approaches, the server behind the counter says: 'What's up?' In so doing, the server is signalling to you that as you are next in line, they are now available to take your order. Indeed, few in their right mind would take this utterance as a genuine, let alone heartfelt, enquiry about their well-being. Imagine the surprise, of customers and servers alike, if upon hearing this I launched into a diatribe on the miseries of my life.

Whether we are aware of it or not, if you or I found ourselves exposed to these words in exactly this context, we wouldn't merely interpret what the server's words commonly mean; we would also be making judgements about what the words mean in this particular setting. This includes understanding our respective roles: mine (or yours) as the customer, and the speaker's as an employee of a fast-food restaurant – the person responsible for taking my (or your) order. And in light of that, we also compute what the speaker's probable communicative intention is in making the utterance – presumably they are not moved to enquire about my or your general well-being because one of us appears to be a bit down in the dumps.

What I am saying is that meaning is anything but a stable residue that can be neatly wrapped up in language, and unpacked, as prescribed by the Conduit Metaphor. Meaning is a process that takes place in the here and now of communication; it is dynamic and mutable, rather than being a thing that lies outside us, objectively, in the world, like lamp posts, buildings and mountains. In terms of human communication, there is no such thing as a view from nowhere: what our words mean is always a consequence of person, place and time.[36]

Any system of communication is tied to its context of use – this is as true of Emoji as it is of language. For instance, emojis have given new grist to the double entendre mill in the realm of so-called sexting – the sending of erotic or sexually explicit text messages. For instance, the aubergine (UK) or eggplant (US) emoji, in certain circles, has become a convenient emoji representation for the male sexual organ; while a variety of plant and flower emojis, including the peach emoji, are used for female genitalia.

The perceived resemblance between the aubergine emoji and the male anatomy provides a visual metaphor that might, between the romantically involved, provide an amusing and less forthright way of conveying what the sender has in mind. One intrepid American entrepreneur has taken advantage of this emoji-driven metaphor, hitting the headlines in the process, by setting up an actual 'Mail an eggplant' service. For just a few dollars (or pounds – you choose your currency), customers can have an eggplant, with a personalised message adorning the vegetable, mailed anonymously anywhere in the world. As the company's publicity puts it: 'Our customers are using the phallic fruit to make up, break up and celebrate life,' with example messages such as 'Suck on this. We are finished,' or 'Happy birthday you naughty little boy'.[37] Figure 8 in the picture section shows another message from the company website. To date, over 16,000 saucy eggplants have been paid for and dispatched since the site's launch.

But here's the point: emojis for fruit or flowers only work as visual metaphors for male and female genitalia in context. When the discussion is about food, then aubergines and peaches remain types of fruit and veg. But when the sender and addressee are romantically involved, or when the conversation is flirtatious in nature, then the context coerces a different meaning, one that is more sexual in nature. And if the secondary, erotic meaning, in the case of the aubergine, is used frequently enough, then over time this can become a convention. It can even come to be viewed by a significant subset of emoji users as the primary meaning of the aubergine. And with its mantle as 'the rudest fruit in town', as one journalist has described the aubergine,[38] this shift in meaning has consequences for how the aubergine is viewed more generally. For instance, in 2015, when Instagram introduced a means of searching for Instagram posts using emojis, users quickly noticed that the aubergine emoji had been blocked. While Instagrammers could search for more innocent fruit, such as bananas, the offending aubergine was just too suggestive. As one jocular newspaper caption put it: 'Is that an emoji in your Instagram feed, or are you just happy to see me?'[39] Instagram has subsequently revoked its ban on the aubergine, perhaps fearing notoriety as an uncool nanny-platform, and for raising the spectre of censorship.

In fact, their metaphoric aptness is a common way in which emojis can shift their meanings in different contexts. Sometimes this can simply employ a pre-existing linguistic metaphor. For instance, a common way of talking about a huckster or charlatan is to refer to them as a shark. But the hackneyed expression, *My lawyer is a shark*, is altogether more amusing when conveyed using an emoji: My lawyer is a 🦈 .

But in cases like this, the visual metaphor is not based on perceived physical resemblance, unlike in the aubergine case. After all, it is not the case that by virtue of being a lawyer one has to physically resemble a shark. The perceived resemblance, in the lawyer-as-shark case, is not perceptual, but functional. The aggressive and unseemly behaviour of sharks, as they circle their prey before going in for the literal kill, is analogous, at least in some people's experiences, to the behaviour of lawyers in legal contexts.

Yet another way in which emojis exhibit variation in meaning comes from their depiction across different software systems. While Unicode sets the international standard, with 'code points' assigned to any individual emoji, each operating system (Apple, Google, Samsung etc.) designs and presents images in slightly different ways. To illustrate, and in keeping with the crime theme of the chapter, take the gun emoji. While Unicode specifies the existence of a (hand) gun emoji, each software developer designs and renders it in a proprietary way. Figure 9 in the picture section illustrates some of the ways in which the gun emoji is represented across platforms.

Microsoft represents it as a revolver, while it's a pistol for LG, and for iOS 10.0 it's a water pistol. But the consequence of these different visual depictions is that the emoji represents a slightly different concept on each platform; and this leads to variation in what emoji users actually perceive when receiving or sending the gun emoji. It matters a lot whether I receive a pistol versus a water pistol depiction as this changes what I take the image to represent and hence mean. After all, the New York District Attorney would not, presumably, have issued an arrest warrant had Osiris Aristy posted water-pistol variants of the gun emoji rather than the actual images he employed.

The encyclopaedic mind

So, let's examine in a bit more detail why different depictions for ostensibly the same emoji – that of a gun – lead to variation in meaning. Of course, it's blindingly obvious that an image of a water pistol calls to mind a harmless toy, while an image of a revolver calls to mind a weapon that can unleash lethal force. But the fact is that, just as context influences what an emoji means, what we already know about what an emoji is *supposed* to represent also contributes to its meaning.

Any meaningful element in a system of communication amounts to a symbol. A symbol is a physical representation that has a widely accepted or conventional meaning associated with it. For instance, in English, the sound elements /k/, /æ/ and /t/, arranged in a specified order, provide the spoken symbol for *cat*. And the glyph gives an emoji symbol for the same idea.

But while symbols – words or emojis – represent meanings, the meanings we carry around with us in our heads are a far cry from the neat, circumscribed definitions that you or I might find in a standard dictionary. In fact, emojis, like words, represent complex bodies of meaning that are rich and multifaceted. The body of knowledge that a word or an emoji relates to is better likened to an encyclopaedia than a dictionary. And it is precisely because we have this rich encyclopaedic knowledge that different depictions of the same emoji have slightly different meanings for us.

To get a better sense of how this works, let's begin with language, before returning to the case of the gun emoji. Take, for instance, the item you are engaging with right now: a book; let's explore all the things you know about books. We know that conventional books involve physical materials, including a cover, pages, a binding and so forth. Sometimes the binding is made from paper, and sometimes hard-backed cloth. And the more materials used, the heavier the book. In terms of the number of words, pages and size of the font, a book can be longer or shorter – not in the sense of its physical dimensions: no one gets fooled, when I say that a book was *too long*, into thinking I'm complaining that it's too long for my tape measure! We also know that books are produced by writers of various kinds – novelists, biographers, kiss-and-tell celebrities, and so on – for various purposes: for the sake of art, to entertain, to inform, to make money. The authors have literary agents who represent them, and editors who work with the text and the writers, and on occasion with writer's block. We know that books are consumed by readers, who must learn how to read, over several years, as a child. I could go on. The point is that we have a huge body of knowledge concerning what a book is, what it entails, what books are for and how we interact with them. Far from our mental idea or concept of 'book' having a simple, dictionary-like definition, it comes in the form of an interconnected and relatively diffuse body of knowledge – even for something as ostensibly straightforward as our idea of what a book is. This is the very nature of a concept.

But what is especially important is that the meaning of the word *book* varies, drawing on different aspects of our encyclopaedic knowledge, when primed by the surrounding language. Think about it for second: *a heavy book* refers to the weight of the book, *a long book* refers to the time it takes to read it, while *a boring book* refers to whether the content holds the reader's attention or not.

Now here's a slightly different example. While *book* refers to a broad body of encyclopaedic knowledge, there are also cases where the same body of encyclopaedic knowledge is referred to by several words. For instance, the English words *shore* and *coast* both refer to the strip of land that borders a body of water. But our encyclopaedic knowledge for this strip of land tells us that the same strip can be approached from the water (*shore*), or land (*coast*). And it is for this reason that a trip that is *coast-to-coast* is across land, while one that is *shore-to-shore* is across water. Part of what *shore* and *coast* convey is the perspective from which the strip of land is being viewed. And this is only possible because of the diffuse, encyclopaedic knowledge that we carry around with us about how bodies of water and land are connected and related.

It is for this reason that even simple expressions can be ambiguous. For instance, the expression *a red pen* has at least two possible, and quite distinct, interpretations. It can refer to a pen whose outer casing is red (but which produces, for instance, black writing), or a pen that contains red ink, producing red writing (but which has a black casing). Each interpretation expresses a different piece of our encyclopaedic knowledge. We require additional language in order to clearly understand what the speaker means.

Now let's return to Emoji and guns. Your encyclopaedic knowledge may (or may not) include the difference between a revolver and a pistol – this relates to the way in which the bullets are stored within the weapon and fired. In a revolver there is a revolving cylinder, while in a pistol there is a cartridge, with a spring that pushes the next bullet into the firing chamber. Whether or not you had that distinction – although you do now – you will certainly know that a water pistol expels not bullets, but water. And, whether or not you've ever interacted with guns involving live ammunition, you will certainly know that water pistols cannot cause serious harm, while pistols and revolvers most certainly can.

It is encyclopaedic knowledge such as this that you and I draw upon each time we use, see and respond to a gun emoji. And consequently, it is because there are different representations for ostensibly the same emoji, each of which calls up different aspects of what we know about guns, that diverging images give rise to different meanings.

It's what I mean
(not what I say) that counts

In the wild, many species of animal use a physical form of communication to advertise their hidden dangers: they use colours, sounds and even odours to signal their unpalatability to potential predators. The yellow and black colours of a bumble bee mean danger, don't touch: a small child need only be stung once to quickly adapt their behaviour and develop a sudden fear of the buzzing bee.

The pioneering nineteenth-century evolutionary biologist Sir Edward Bagnall Poulton coined the term *aprosematism* to account for this phenomenon – the term derives from the ancient Greek meaning 'away signal'. Writing in his 1890 treatise on the subject – which applied Darwinian theory to animal colouration – Poulton explains: 'When an animal possesses an unpleasant attribute, it is often to its advantage to advertise the fact as publicly as possible. In this way it escapes a great deal of experimental "tasting".'[40]

But while we might speak loosely of bees communicating their unsavoury qualities through natural advertising, this is not what we usually mean by 'communication'; at least not in common parlance. A bee's bright colours mean danger; but individual bees aren't doing anything deliberate: a bee is not 'choosing' to warn you or me to stay away; after all, it was born that way. The fact that some species have danger written all over them is simply a consequence of an evolutionary co-adaptation to the biological niche they inhabit, including the learning capacities of would-be predators.

In contrast, the hallmark of human communication is the recognition of an intentional signal, understood as an attempt to convey a particular message.[41] Intentional signals come in a wide variety of forms, from the red, amber and green of traffic lights to the bell rings used by conductors on the omnibuses, trams and trains of yesteryear; on the old London Routemaster buses from my childhood, one ring from the conductor told the driver to stop, and two rings meant go. Such communicative systems are intentional in the sense that we all recognise them as conveying a particular meaning – they are expressly employed to communicate specific messages. And more than that, as minded creatures, equipped with the power of interpreting the signals of others as meaningful, we act accordingly. There's a causal relationship between a red traffic light and our behaviour – we stop when we see a red signal, at least most of us do, and most of the time.[42] And social sanctions enforce this causal relationship; going through a red light is a traffic violation and can incur a fine or worse.

Communication not only involves a signal, deliberately produced, to signify a specific, widely known meaning. Crucially, it is also recognised as such by other members of a given community. And this starts to get to the heart of the matter. What we mean is often not what we say, in the sense of what our words literally convey. Indeed, much of the time, what we mean amounts to interpreting what lies behind our words: the communicative intention that underpins the words. Much of what we do when we interact with others, therefore, is try to work out what their words actually mean.

Nowhere is this truer, perhaps, than in the realm of romantic relationships. One commentator, advising men on how to interpret what their female partners say, makes precisely this observation: 'Many relationship missteps men make have to do with not knowing when to take a statement or question from their significant others at face value, and when to dig around for a deeper meaning.'[43] Expressions such as 'We need to talk' or 'Do whatever you want', for experienced relationship watchers, don't actually mean what they say. Correctly understanding that the former actually means 'I need to talk; you need to listen', while the latter means 'This is a test of your judgement, after all you should know me well enough by now to know that I will not be fine with what you are doing', not only helps avoid miscommunication, but may even save a relationship in the process.

If we're to correctly understand that communicative intention, we need to go beyond the words. Non-verbal cues – a wink or a smile – help us figure out what someone means, what the intentional signal might be, lying behind their words. And in the context of digital communication, here Emoji makes a powerful contribution.

Take the banal expression: 'I tripped and banged my head on the cupboard.' If you send an SMS to your friend, partner or colleague, they might not be clear on whether to sympathise or laugh; the words don't actually convey what you mean. However, putting a sad face at the end of the expression provides a non-verbal cue, a metacomment, showing us how to interpret the words: 'I'm in pain.' But a tears of joy emoji tells us that the sender finds the situation funny: 'I'm such a buffoon'.

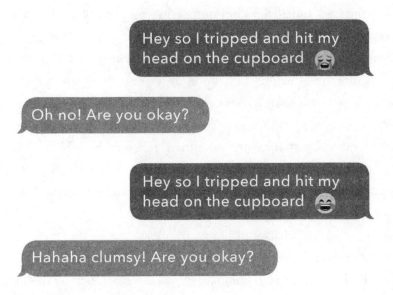

How emojis can reveal the meaning behind words.[44]

Communication in Technicolor

Communicative signals come in all shapes and sizes: they can be gestures, as when I point to something, like a specific pastry in a baker's shop to show that, while I do want a croissant, I want the one without the burnt edges. They can be a facial grimace, or a shrug to signal: *dunno*. Alternatively, we can cough to signal to our comrade in arms to keep quiet in a tricky situation. The point is that communicative signals are multimodal – they make use of different modes, for purposes of communication, which converge on a particular communicative intention.[45] When we point we use the gestural mode; when we cough we use the paralinguistic mode; when we compose a letter, writing in neat, joined-up calligraphy with a fine pen, we use the linguistic mode; and when we adorn our letter with a hand-drawn love heart to our beloved, we are using the visual mode. And adding a squirt of perfume, with the dramatic panache straight out of a nineteenth-century romantic novel, we are using the olfactory mode.

A mode, then, concerns a particular type of information. But importantly, the same mode of information can be conveyed using more than one medium – a medium being a channel by which the information can be represented. For instance, the linguistic mode can be conveyed via the oral-aural medium when we speak; via the manual gestural-visual medium by users of sign languages; by the written-textual medium when we write or type; and even the 2D-visual, as in the case of visual languages (I will discuss an example of a visual language, Blissymbolics, later in the book). Moreover, some modes can be conveyed using the same medium of expression. For instance, facial expressions, such as smiling, frowning or looking sad; hand and arm gesticulations, the sort of gestures that accompany speech; and body posture, like walking upright when happy and slumped when down in the dumps – these are all expressed by the same kinesic-visual medium (kinesics has to do with body movements, and is a subject to which we will return in Chapter 4). The table below provides a summary of some of the most important modes of communication, and their channels of representation.

A fundamental design feature of human communication is that it is multimodal in nature – we use, and require, multiple modes to signal intentions and create meaning, with different modes contributing different sorts of meaning to the whole. Our multimodal communicative signals provide complementary types of information, conveyed via different channels, converging on a rich, and often complex, communicative intention. In this way, communicative intentions are always multifaceted. But due to the complementary and partially overlapping communicative cues provided by the multiple modes, they are understood straightforwardly by their recipient.

This is especially true when we engage in face-to-face interaction.[46] How someone feels about what they are saying, or the person they are saying it to, more often than not comes from modes other than the linguistic.

One consequence of the digital age is that everyday social interaction – in home, educational and professional settings – is not merely the preserve of spoken exchanges, either face-to-face or over the phone. Increasingly, digital communication is replacing aspects of our spoken interactions, especially among the young. Data from the UK suggests that

Mode (information type)	Example	Medium (channel of representation)
Linguistic	Spoken language	Oral-aural
Linguistic	Written/typed language	Written-textual
Linguistic	Signed language	Manual gestural-visual
Linguistic	Visuo-pictographic language	2D-visual
Paralinguistic	Voluntary/involuntary sounds, e.g. cry, laughter, sigh, etc.; or speech prosody, e.g. intonation, stress, rhythm, etc.	Oral-aural
Body postural	Body 'language', e.g. shrug, body posture, etc.	Kinesic-visual
Facial expressive	Facial expressions, e.g. frown, smile, etc.; eye gaze, e.g. direction, eye gaze contact, or lack of, etc.	Kinesic-visual
Gesticulated gestural	Gestures that accompany speech	Kinesic-visual
Emblematic gestural	Stand-alone gestures, e.g. thumbs-up emblem	Kinesic-visual
Visuo-pictographic	Emoji, infographics, photographs, etc.	2D-visual
Visuo-artistic	Paintings	2D-visual
Visuo-artistic	Installations, sculptures, physical artefacts, etc.	3D-visual
Olfactory	Smell	Olfaction
Gustatory	Taste	Gustation

The relationship between modes of information and channels of representation.

today's six-year-olds have equivalent levels of digital technology know-how to the average forty-five-year-old.[47] Moreover, today's adults – sixteen years of age and older – spend on average nearly twenty-two hours per week online. This is more than double what it was a decade earlier.[48] As so much of our daily interaction with others is now transacted online, in order to be an effective communicator in the digital realm we require some of the same sorts of multimodal cues that are available in face-to-face communication.

Emoji offers a burst of colour using the 2D-visual mode and works in conjunction with the linguistic mode to communicate meaning. When Osiris Aristy posted revolver emojis, pointing at an emoji depicting a police officer, one, perhaps reasonable, inference was that the teenager was threatening gun violence against the NYPD. But the emojis didn't appear in isolation. On the contrary, they were part of a multimodal message.

Osiris Aristy
January 4 at 12:55pm ·

I keep in touch with all my niqqas yea.. They all doing fine free my brother he doing his bid right along RNS 🔫🔫💨👮👮👮FREE EMONEY Erick Santiago

One of Osiris Aristy's public Facebook posts.[49]

In the post, the linguistic mode provides information about the issues relating to race; for instance Aristy uses the term *niqqa*, which is an 'eye-dialect' form of the more controversial term *nigger*; the spelling *niqqa* is sometimes used to avoid posts being reported for using a potentially derogatory term. In the post, Aristy also alludes to the US criminal justice system: *free my brother* is a call to free an associate of Aristy's. The abbreviation RNS stands for 'Real Nigga Shit', and is used to add emphasis: *No bullshit/I'm deadly serious about this*. But the emojis – using the 2D-visual medium – provide complementary information that add to the textual. The cop emoji followed by gun emojis might amount to a threat of vengeance against the NYPD. And indeed, when his home was raided, Aristy was found to have a .38 calibre Smith & Wesson revolver.

In issuing the arrest warrant, Aristy's emojis were evaluated by the NY District Attorney as declaring a particular communicative intention. And the meaning behind the emojis were evaluated as expressing a similar intention to that expressed by the words *gonna shoot a cop*. But while the emojis were assessed as expressing an alleged threat, the communicative intention arose from a combination of information conveyed using different modes; it's precisely because of the context provided via the textual mode that the emojis could be interpreted as, allegedly, making a threat to harm NY's finest. The legal judgment by the District Attorney resulted from the interpretation of the multimodal nature of the Facebook post.

Ultimately, who would have thought that Aristy's indignant Facebook posts would have caught the eye of the NY District Attorney? But in today's global village, we communicate not just with words, but in

Technicolor. And that, in itself, is a salutary lesson; in terms of digital communication, others are liable to interpret our intentions as much from our emojis as the words we type – emojis convey meaning; they can and will be used in a court of law against you.[50]

Everyday mind control

So if meaning is as much a matter of what the speaker intends as what they literally say, what is the function of our communicative intentions? What is meaning for?

We recognise other members of our species as intentional agents. What I mean by this is that we understand that others have thoughts, feelings, wishes and desires more or less similar to our own. It is precisely because of this that when you see a stranger crying, you perceive them to be sad. And when they smile you assume they are happy. And in doing this you are engaging in a form of mind-reading, a consequence of recognising that others have feelings, thoughts, desires that approximate your own, that they know things, like you do, and can dissemble and even lie. While this seems like child's play, understanding that others have minds, wishes, thoughts and feelings, more or less like our own, is beyond the ken of all, or nearly all, other species. There are perhaps a few exceptions, especially chimpanzees and pygmy chimpanzees, and some birds such as ravens and scrub jays, which have rudimentary mind-reading abilities, and possibly other mammals, including dogs.[51]

If I choose to deliberately bump into someone, I can cause them physical pain, which influences how they feel – sadness, anguish, resentment. But in addition, I can affect their thoughts and feelings by my intentional communicative behaviour – by the words I utter, even the most banal: *Shut the door on your way out, please.* As my addressee knows me to be an intentional agent, they recognise the behaviour as intentional, and seek to infer the message behind my intentional action: *I desire that they respect my wishes, by ensuring the door is closed on their way out.*

In this way, my mind is symbiotically linked to those around me: we all share a level of intentionality with our fellow human beings, a benign form of everyday mind control. Not only do we recognise and empathise with their joy and suffering, we can also influence their mental states with our intentional actions. Blowing a kiss to someone signals the idea that we wish them to consider themselves kissed. And waving goodbye signals that we bid them farewell. The cooperative basis for communication is built upon a shared awareness of others as sentient beings with whom we have a broad spectrum of mental states in common.

The crux of the matter is that this sharing of intentionality, the essential elixir of communication, enables us to coordinate our interaction and actions way beyond the capability of any other species. After all, by recognising that we share a range of mental attitudes with others, and that we can influence the mental states of others, we can pool our mental resources. And pooling resources helps us to better enhance our material lives – starting with the primary goals of all members of our species: food, shelter and the opportunity to reproduce being chief among them. And beyond that, in modern societies, the niceties of a reliable broadband connection, a TV that works, and all the creature comforts that we take for granted, are better achieved by collaborating. In short, sharing intentionality provides us with the potential to pool our collective resources. But the pooling of our collective smarts, so that each can play their part in enabling us to achieve our individual and shared goals, entails cooperation. In essence, a communication system allows us to get stuff done!

The power of communicative systems, like language, and yes, Emoji, derives from this powerful form of everyday mind control: recognising the communicative intentions of others as an attempt to influence our thoughts and feelings. It requires joint intentionality: a mutual understanding that we have broadly similar mental states that can be influenced. But then, the purpose of communication is to enable us to influence the minds of others. And by this, I'm not talking about the honeyed words of politicians seeking your vote; nor do I mean the clever marketing slogan, tag line or hook. A run-of-the-mill *Wipe those muddy boots before you come in, please* is an attempt to have you conform to my wishes, and hence, to have an aspect of the world suit my own desired state of affairs. And public acts of communication, such as the solemn pronouncement by a member of the clergy, saying, *I now pronounce you husband and wife*, again influences the mental states of the newlyweds, as well as all around them. Marriage is created by the words, by the speech act,[52] as well as the spoken vows the couple make to one another, witnessed by friends and family. And these actions, mediated by language, guide our subsequent behaviour and expectations with respect to the newlyweds. Far from marriage being something that lies outside us, in objective reality, it is a construct created, in part, by language; and more precisely, by the cultural web of knowledge we all share: our mental states, enacted and reinforced by language, help create a social reality that guides our behaviour.[53]

Whether you want it or not, we are born to communicate. Ignoring the intentional overtures of others, even the unsolicited ones, does not absolve you, in the eyes of the world, from recognising their communicative intentions – the defence of being a hermit is no defence at all. Choosing to set aside the very principle of cooperation that amounts to the modus operandi of our species just makes others see you as difficult and moody.

Thought crime and the case of the emoji that isn't there

If the function of communication is to enable everyday mind control, then having the power to shape our means of communication may, potentially, go further and take us into the realm of thought control. Nowhere is this clearer than when a system of communication is controlled, not by individual users, but by large corporations, as is the case for Emoji.

One consequence of Apple having changed the depiction of the gun emoji with its update in iOS 10.0, in September 2016, is that its users are safeguarded from an ill-judged message or status update. Of course, an altogether different question is whether this amounts to a form of thought control, à la Newspeak, from George's Orwell's classic novel *1984*. In Orwell's totalitarian state, the removal of particular words made it possible for the state to control the communicative intentions of its citizens and, arguably, thought itself. All things being equal, language is actually less prone than Emoji to the sort of thought control that Orwell imagined, as it evolves via the changing use of individuals.

The ethics at play here are particularly pertinent for Emoji. As we already began to see in the previous chapter, Emoji is unlike a natural language in that it is controlled by powerful multinationals whose representatives sit on the various Unicode committees. Even more powerful are the software developers such as Apple, Google and Microsoft, which interpret the Unicode code points, and design what a particular emoji looks like on their platforms.

Osiris Aristy has not been the only person to have been accused of issuing threats with emojis. In recent times, other high-profile court cases have featured evidence involving emojis. In the United States, an elementary school in Colorado was shut, and pupils evacuated, after the school received an email containing bomb, gun and knife emojis. It later transpired that the message was not, in fact, a bomb threat, but an innocent mistake by an eight-year-old girl from a neighbouring school – the email also contained non-threatening emojis such as chickens.[54] Elsewhere, a twelve-year-old girl from Fairfax, Virginia, faced criminal charges for threatening her school: she posted on Instagram bomb, knife and gun emojis with the word 'killing', and the sinister sounding 'meet me in the library Tuesday'.[55] In the UK, a Conservative Member of Parliament, Craig Mackinlay, received an emoji death threat – including gun and knife emojis. This was promptly reported to the police, making headlines when British law enforcement approved the MP's request for a panic button to be installed in his constituency office.[56] And perhaps most seriously of all, in France, a twenty-something man was even imprisoned for three months for sending an emoji death threat – a handgun emoji – to his former girlfriend, leaving her in fear for her life.[57] This spate of well-publicised death threats using Emoji no doubt helped trigger Apple's decision to change its depiction of the gun emoji from a revolver to a water pistol.

This returns us to the issue of whether it is permissible for a software developer to restrict what we can search for, and express, electronically, that we first discussed earlier with Instagram and its ban on the aubergine search. Presumably, an emoji user can't interpret someone sending a water pistol as intentionally signalling a death threat. But is the function of a software developer to limit what people can and cannot signal using emojis? By changing the representation for the gun emoji, Apple is, effectively, constraining what its users can use Emoji to express. Given that a communicative system has implications for the thoughts and ideas we can evoke in the minds of others, then we can reasonably ask whether this amounts to a form of thought control. And while this intervention may be well meaning it is arguably a form of censorship. Of course, a huge corporation, with shareholders to protect, might take the view that subscribers are paying for a service – Emoji does not have the same status as a natural form of communication, such as a language like English – hence Apple can do what it wants, more or less, with its proprietary versions of the Unicode-prescribed emojis. Moreover, arrests and criminal convictions involving emojis sent via the Apple platform may be bad for the company's reputation, which the execs that run the company may feel is sufficient justification for changing the handgun emoji to resemble a harmless toy. But for anyone who believes in freedom of self-expression and the power of digital systems of communication, overseen by a not-for-profit organisation – Unicode – then this establishes a dangerous precedent. An individual company is influencing the way many of us communicate, and express ourselves, when using its proprietary emoji images, in service of its public-relations imperatives.

Such a move also creates a legal minefield: how do the police and the judiciary respond when the sender, using an Apple device, sends their addressee a water pistol emoji, knowing their recipient uses a device that displays the emoji as a lethal weapon? Was there criminal intent here? After all, what was sent was an image of a water-squirting toy. But a threat may nevertheless be both perceived and real.

A further consequence of this sort of pictographic variation means that there are also emerging 'dialects' of Emoji. As each platform has a single form for the same emoji, which is specific to the platform, then we can think of Apple subscribers as using a slightly different, albeit a mutually intelligible, variety compared to, say, Samsung subscribers.

The reach of software developers even extends beyond the way in which individual emojis are displayed: they also have the power to ban emojis from seeing the light of day. An example of this was the proposed rifle emoji. A number of new emojis were due to be inaugurated as part of a 2017 Unicode update, to celebrate summer and winter sports. Emojis for a curling stone and a sled, to signify Olympic winter sports, along with emojis for water polo and judo were approved. But at the last minute, the rifle emoji was unceremoniously dropped, even after having made it through the tough vetting process – the rifle was meant to symbolise the biathlon, a winter sport involving skiing followed by shooting at targets. Indeed, the summary removal of the proposed rifle emoji was so late in the day that it had already been assigned a Unicode code point. Nevertheless, the decision was taken not to give the code point emoji representation.

Those in the know allege that Apple representatives sitting on Unicode led the revolt against the rifle emoji.[58] According to one report, at the meeting where the rifle's emoji status was being discussed, Apple 'told the consortium it would not support a rifle on its platforms and asked for it not to be made into an emoji'.[59] By indicating what amounted to a boycott, Apple was, in effect, applying pressure upon the other members of Unicode to blackball an approved emoji. This led to the bizarre consequence that an emoji that had been sanctioned by Unicode was subsequently denied emoji representation – becoming the emoji that isn't there.

While commentators often decry an epidemic of gun crime in the United States, pointing to the many thousands killed and injured from gun violence each year, is this sufficient justification to block a rifle emoji? Gun violence is clearly abhorrent. And the reasons for it, especially in the somewhat unique context of the United States, are a matter for strong measures by the appropriate authorities; but it is less clear how this provides international tech companies with the moral authority to restrict which sort of emojis can be encoded by Unicode as a consequence. The ethical issue concerns us all: is freedom of expression subject to constraint because some social media users may misuse proprietary emojis to threaten and intimidate? For some the answer may be yes. But I would counter that imposing bans on an emoji for such reasons is, at least in principle, no different from the pernicious totalitarianism of the thought control depicted in George Orwell's dystopian classic.

Communicating without words

I began this chapter by considering the Conduit Metaphor as a model for how communication works. But as we've seen, communication entails more than packing ideas into language as a conduit, which can be unpacked revealing their inner semantic core. In fact, language is only one means – albeit an extremely effective one – of facilitating communication. Language itself is not even necessary for communication. The following demonstration proves the point nicely.

Two volunteers are drawn from the audience and asked to stand on stage with their backs to one another, so that they cannot see the other person. Each volunteer is given a sheet of paper with the following words printed: *tree, predator, fruit, rain*. On the two sheets, the words are arranged in a different order. Each volunteer is asked to take it in turns to provide clues as to the words on their list. The person guessing the word, while knowing the options, doesn't know which order the words appear in. The demonstrator then explains the rules of the game: the person whose turn it is to provide clues may make any sound they choose, but may not use language. And as the person guessing cannot see the other person, they have no visual clues either.

Invariably, the person providing clues chooses a growling sound for *predator*, a munching sound for *fruit*, a plipp sound for *rain*, and a gentle whoosh sound for *tree*. And very quickly, the words are correctly guessed.

While impressive – and I've seen this demonstrated at first-hand, while presenting at a digital communication event[60] – you might object that it nevertheless still relies on language. After all, both volunteers know the possible set of words they must guess.

So, consider instances of successful communication without any recourse to language. Imagine standing forlornly on a street corner, armed only with a map, completely lost in a foreign city. A passer-by comes up to you jabbering away in a language you don't understand. With smiles and gestures, you're able to communicate where you're trying to get to. And by pointing out the route on the map, your Good Samaritan shows you the way to your destination.

And a real-life example makes a similar point. In 2001, a contestant on the UK TV quiz show *Who Wants to Be a Millionaire?* hit the headlines when he was convicted of winning the £1,000,000 prize by deception. Aided by an accomplice, Major Charles Ingram cheated his way to the prize. The game show works by a question being posed, and four possible answers being read out. Major Ingram's accomplice, in the audience, coughed when the quiz show host read out the correct answer. Later, with the help of acoustic analysis by the TV company, the major was found out.

Similarly, if there's damage to the areas of the brain associated with language, a condition known as aphasia can arise. There are two main types of aphasia, one in which a patient is impaired in their ability to produce language, and another in which patients are unable to understand language. Aphasia can be caused by brain trauma due to tumour or head injury. But despite the loss of the ability to produce or understand language, patients still retain normal IQ, they can still ride a bike, tie their own shoelaces, drive a car, and function more or less effectively. More importantly, they are still able to communicate their wishes, feelings and desires: gesture, facial expressions and body language are powerful communicative cues. It's simply that language is no longer available as a mode of communication.

Perhaps an even more powerful example comes from research on what has been dubbed 'home-sign'. In the United States, the psychologist Susan Goldin-Meadow has studied the deaf children of hearing parents.[61] For a variety of reasons, some such children have not been taught American Sign Language, the sign language of the deaf community of the United States. Nevertheless, in many cases, these children have created their own, self-developed system of gestured communication. It is this that Goldin-Meadow dubs home-sign. Home-sign is a rudimentary system of communication in which the children develop basic vocabulary items and grammatical markers from gestures. For instance, two hands held together making a flapping gesture might indicate a bird, while shaking the head while gesturing might serve a negation function, equivalent to saying *none* or *not*. What this shows is that expressing communicative intentions is a powerful impulse in our species.[62]

The point, of course, is communication can be enabled ad hoc – without recourse to language or another conventional system of communication. The case of coughing is particularly instructive. While a cough can be a reflex behaviour, it can also be an intentional signal used cooperatively to convey a particular message. Some types of communication do, of course, require language. Making a telephone call, producing and reading a newspaper article, or a radio news bulletin are primarily constituted by language. But the telltale signs that someone is romantically interested in you may rely almost entirely on non-verbal cues, especially when you, love-struck, lock eyes with a stranger across a crowded room.

While language doubtless massively amplifies our communicative potential, what enables communication in the first place is something else: understanding others as intentional agents who produce intentional signals that we recognise as such. We use these signals in order to influence the minds, actions and behaviour of others. And it was this very issue that was put to a grand jury, when they were asked by the New York District Attorney to indict Osiris Aristy for an alleged terroristic threat made using emojis. The grand jury considered whether the emojis used conveyed the intentional signal alleged in the indictment documents; did Aristy, by posting his emojis, mean to incite or threaten gun crime? Ultimately, the grand jury decided that no terroristic threat was intended; and they declined to indict. But in the end, the hallmark of communication, the expression of an intentional signal, is what makes Emoji such an apt means of communicating ideas in the digital age. It serves up relatively complex ideas in simple glyphs. While emoji crime provides, albeit on the face of it, an unlikely lens into the nature of communication, it also reveals how Emoji works as a powerful system of communication. And that should impress us all.

3

What's in a Word?

Each year Oxford Dictionaries, one of the world's leading arbiters of English language usage, selects a word that has become prominent or notable in some way during the past twelve months and anoints it Word of the Year. The word is carefully selected by thorough examination of how often it's used, involving complex statistical procedures that analyse millions and millions of words – 2.5 billion of them to be precise – from a huge collection of language known as the Oxford English Corpus. This Corpus harvests authentic twenty-first-century English from the internet, capturing text of all types, ranging from novels, magazines, newspapers, and even blogs, emails and social media. Next, dictionary-writers, consultants and other experts debate the case for each potential Word of the Year, before anguishing, finally, over an eventual winner. The duly garlanded word is thereby imbued with special significance, saying as much about the times we live in – and who we have become as individuals and a society – as it does about how often we used it over the course of the previous twelve months. For instance, past holders of the position include *vape*, *selfie* and *omnishambles*, revealing key aspects of a particular year's zeitgeist.

It doesn't have to be a word coined in the previous twelve months. It might have been kicking around for some time. But commentators and language users alike take a keen interest in the deliberations of the wise men and women from an institution as illustrious as Oxford University Press. After all, language is the tissue that connects us with others: it reflects our social reality, which it also has a hand in creating – we use language to get married, to quarrel, to make up afterwards, and (should that fail) to get divorced. And indeed, the great English word is, for many, the most sacred cornerstone of our 'proudly barbaric yet deeply civilised' tongue, and for others the 'shameless whore' (according to Stephen Fry).[63] English is the prism through which the genius of our literary giants – Chaucer, Shakespeare, Jane Austen, Dickens, D.H. Lawrence, James Joyce, T.S. Eliot, Bob Dylan and many others – is able to shine. And our love affair with language is evidenced in its use and abuse: from the twisted, knifed words of the playground bully to the love sonnets of our most revered poets.

The announcement of the Word of the Year often initiates debate, but the 2015 winner provoked a quite extraordinary outburst of emotion, with reactions ranging from bemusement to outright anger. Why? Because it was not, in fact, a word at all, but rather an emoji. To be precise, the 'face with tears of joy' emoji 😂 . Writing in the *Guardian*, journalist

Hannah Jane Parkinson (doubtless speaking for many others) branded the decision 'ridiculous'.[64] For Parkinson, and many of the language mavens out there, it's 'ridiculous' because it's not even a word in the first place. Surely, surely, this was a stunt, dreamed up by clever marketing executives bent on demonstrating just how hip Oxford Dictionaries can be.

Of course, it's easy to dismiss Oxford Dictionaries' decision out of hand. After all, an emoji is, self-evidently, not a word. But is such derision really warranted? After all, we live in a digital age, and the media we use to connect and communicate with our nearest and dearest, as well as a virtual world of friends and followers, surely requires an evolution if not revolution in our systems of communication. And a communicative system, such as Emoji, is an adaptation to this most recent arena of human interaction. Emoji gets the job done when the tried and tested interpersonal cues that oil spoken interaction are impossible or absent. But is Emoji, which, as we saw in Chapter 2, most definitely meets the criterion for a communicative system, so different from language itself?

If we set aside our educated bias that perceives the canonical English word as sacrosanct, we are left with some rather interesting questions. In our landscape of contemporary digital communication, what does the decision to name an emoji Word of the Year for 2015 reveal about the nature and changing status of language? What does the seemingly unstoppable rise of Emoji mean for the shifting sands of human communication? And is the good old-fashioned English word really in peril?

To be, or not to be ... a word?

In certain respects, the shortlist for the 2015 Word of the Year was unremarkable. The other shortlisted words actually were, well, words. Moreover, they reflected the times. Several of the words related to digital technology, for instance *ad blocker* (a piece of software that prevents adverts from appearing on web pages) and *dark web* (the nether regions of the internet, obscured from the Big Brother surveillance of national security agencies, where a shadowy black market deals in everything from illegal drugs to armaments).

Others related to political or humanitarian topics of the day. For instance, *refugee* was also shortlisted, a reflection of its 110 per cent increase in usage over the previous twelve months.[65] Humanitarian crises, especially in countries such as Syria and Iraq, during the period led to much public debate by politicians and the written and broadcast media, which partly accounted for the upsurge in usage.

Refugee is a relatively old world. It was borrowed by English from the French *refugié*, meaning to take shelter, and was first applied to French Huguenots moving to England in the 1680s, following religious persecution in their homeland. It retained this meaning of 'someone seeking asylum' until the First World War. The current meaning of 'someone fleeing home' was first applied to inhabitants of the Flanders region of modern-day Belgium who fled west to avoid the trench warfare of the Great War of 1914–18.

Another politically motivated word that cropped up on the shortlist was *Brexit*. This word was coined as early as 2012 by blending the first two letters from *Britain* with *exit*.[66] The word took on new prominence during the course of 2015, following the British Government's European Union (EU) Referendum Act, and paving the way for an in/out referendum on the UK's membership of the EU, which took place in June 2016.

But my favourite conventional item on the shortlist was *lumbersexual* – a compound word formed by combining the first half of *lumberjack* with *sexual*, and standing in opposition to the older term *metrosexual*. *Lumbersexual* began to appear as early as 2008, referring to a specific fashion trend: trendy, urban men who adopt a rugged, outdoor demeanour, and have a particular penchant for red checked shirts and thick beards. The term peaked in the Oxford English Corpus in the first half of 2015. But what stole the show was the eventual winner: the 'face with tears of joy' emoji.

But let's face it. An emoji isn't a word, at least in the conventional sense as understood by journalists and the educated public. To the layperson, a word is a single, meaningful unit of speech or written text. In written text, we know whether something is a word by the white spaces around it. And in spoken language, the prototypical word is marked by intonation strategies, including stress, syllable structure and tempo, by which we can distinguish when one word begins and another ends. Speech prosody provides, in part, the punctuation in speech, a topic I'll return to in the next chapter.

For instance, the *dis-* in *disinformation* is not a single word on this account. It can't stand on its own without a friend to help us figure out what is being *dis*-ed. *Disinformation* is a complex word, made up of component parts: the prefix *dis-* and the free-standing word *information*.

But in spoken language, this faith in a nice, neat definition of a word begins to break down. For instance, what can we say about a contraction like *'ll*, as in *It'll rain tomorrow*: is *'ll* a word? One solution is to say that *'ll* is simply a lazy way of pronouncing *will* – the full word from which we derive the contracted form. But in both written and spoken English *'ll* and *will* occur in different contexts of use: the full form, *will*, is typically reserved for emphasis, and is much less frequent than the contraction. This suggests we actually have two forms: *will* and *'ll*, which are used differently; they amount to two slightly different words.

Things get more complex with other contractions. For instance, *gonna* or *ain't* are contractions of *going to* and *am not* respectively. Indeed, this pattern of reducing several words by telescoping them into one is part and parcel of how English continues to change. While the purist might claim that *gonna* is simply sloppy colloquial English, no one in their right mind would, presumably, sniffily object to the legitimacy of *goodbye* being a bona fide English word. Yet, *goodbye* is the contraction of the standard valedictory term in Shakespeare: *God be with ye. Goodbye* was once the poor man's version of a fuller form. And famous place names, such as the hip English seaside resort Brighton are contractions of longer names, now long gone: the town was known as Bright Helm Stone in Anglo-Saxon times.

In addition, while objectionable for some, the semantic function of *gonna* is quite different from *going to. Gonna* only has a future meaning; a child might say: *I'm gonna be an astronaut when I grow up*. In contrast, *going to* can either refer to motion through space – *I'm going to Land's End* – or to future time. But *gonna*, it seems, cannot convey motion: **I'm gonna Land's End* is ungrammatical (conveyed here, as is the custom in linguistics, by placing an asterisk before the ungrammatical sentence). The contraction *gonna* seems to have made the jump to being a fully fledged word, with a meaning distinct from the original motion meaning associated with the fuller form; this is a conclusion, no doubt, that is an abomination to the self-appointed grammar militia.

With regard to our commonplace definition, where does this leave 'words' in sign language? There are 130 recorded sign languages in the world – although the true figure is likely to be far higher.[67] It has been known since the 1960s that a sign language is the functional equivalent of a spoken language, with a comparable level of semantic and grammatical complexity as any spoken language. In the UK, for instance, British Sign Language (BSL) is the official language of the deaf community, but it is entirely unrelated to American Sign Language (ASL). Indeed, each country typically has its own indigenous sign language. Estimates vary considerably as to the actual number of sign language users. In the UK, for instance, as many as 250,000 people may be conversant to some degree in BSL, a number that includes deaf adults and children as well as some hearing adults who use BSL to communicate with them. There are also different dialects of BSL, in the same way that spoken English, even within the same country, exhibits considerable dialectal variation.

In spoken language, the word *dog*, involves three distinct sound segments sequenced in a particular order. Each sound is produced using various components of the human articulatory tract, including the vocal folds in the voice box, the tongue, lips, mouth, teeth and nasal cavity. The sound system of a spoken language involves manipulating these physical articulators to change the shape of the articulatory tract as air is expelled from the lungs; this produces the set of sounds that constitute the sound inventory of a given spoken language – and languages vary. For instance, languages range from an inventory of a mere eleven distinct sounds, such as Hawaiian and Pirãha – the latter spoken by a tribe in remote Amazonia – to languages with a massive 144 in some African languages.[68]

Analogously, sign languages also involve mobile articulators, which must be positioned and moved correctly in space to produce the requisite signs that populate a given sign language system. For instance, in ASL, the sign for 'think' requires the fingertip to make contact with the forehead. The sign for 'funny' entails the fingertip making contact with the nose. And the sign for 'mirror' requires that the hand be near, and ahead, but not touching the nose. If one sign is replaced by another, or indeed if the sign is incorrectly executed, then a different sign is produced, or no sign is produced at all. So while sign and spoken language make use of different channels for their expression, they both use physical representations – symbols produced using either sound or gesture – to construct words.

From this perspective, an emoji is not so different from a word. An emoji is a single meaningful unit deployed in digital, text-based communication. As Emoji is indeed a system of communication, with the individual emojis having discrete, conventional meanings within this system, emojis have an analogous formal and semantic function to words in spoken, written or signed linguistic communication. Evidence for this comes from situations in which emojis are used to replace an English word in a text message. For instance, when someone writes *Have you fed the cat?* and the word *cat* is replaced with the corresponding emoji: *Have you fed the 🐱?*

I was once chatting with a friend in a Parisian bar. My friend and I were speaking French, but he was also fluent in English. He said: *C'est dure, you know!* This is an example of what linguists refer to as 'code-switching', and is especially prevalent in bilingual communities. In this example, my friend inserted an English expression into the language we were otherwise using in our boozy conversation. And the way in which emojis are sometimes used to replace words in textspeak is in principle no different.

This all reveals that the nature and status of what we take to be a word is not an all-or-nothing affair. Even in English, a word has fuzzy boundaries. And as emojis can be substituted for a word in text-based communication, this begs the question as to whether they can function in word-like ways. This all goes to show that the sneering disdain that many commentators have exhibited towards Oxford Dictionaries' decision is arguably wide of the mark. At best it's ill-informed. And at its worst it's a symptom of the prejudice on the part of some who don't fully understand the nature of human communication and how it's evolving in the digital age.

So what makes a language?

The thing is that different experts have different views on what makes something a language. For some, a language is a system of communication that is passed down from one generation to another. But a language has to start somewhere. For instance, no one would dispute that Esperanto is a language, even though it was invented in the nineteenth century. Today Esperanto even has native speakers, who have learned it as a mother tongue. So if being passed down across the generations is not the hallmark of language, what about learnability? The difficulty here is that any system of communication is, at least in principle, learnable. I can learn Morse Code, or you can learn a rudimentary system of smoke signals – smoke signals amount to one of the oldest systems of communication and have been in use continuously for many thousands of years. They were used by soldiers who manned the Great Wall of China, and are still taught today in the Girl Guide and Boy Scout movements. So learnability is something associated with any system of communication, rather than language specifically. Moreover, systems of communication aren't unique to humans: many other species have rudimentary systems of communication that allow them to warn of danger, or to communicate a desire to play, request food, or to initiate sexual activity.

What actually makes something a language concerns the way in which it is organised. And it is the unique nature of this organisation – which appears to be a skill known only to humans – that allows us to express complex and subtle ideas that cannot be expressed using other systems of communication. For instance, as the celebrated philosopher Bertrand Russell once pithily observed: '*No matter how eloquently a dog may bark, he cannot tell you that his parents were poor but honest.*'[69] The point is, of course, that language goes beyond any other system of communication in facilitating the articulation of complex and subtle ideas. Without language, the lowly dog, for all its canine emotional eloquence, is unable to express familial attributes.

Language achieves this because of the way it is organised into meaningful units – such as words – and because it has a system of rules – a grammar – that enables us to compose our words in a way that expresses ideas of great complexity, from the gnawing ache of unrequited love to a banal comment on the weather.

Let's begin, then, with vocabulary. While English today has, on some counts, well over a million words, speakers typically know far fewer, with the average vocabulary of an adult person estimated to range between 10,000 and 30,000 words.[70] In the 1930s, the British linguist and psychologist Charles K. Ogden advocated a Basic English movement. Ogden claimed that we can express ourselves effectively using a mere 1,500 words, made up of 850 basic words, plus others of international origin as well as scientific terms. Winston Churchill, no less, was reputed to be an enthusiast. Indeed, the suite of Oxford dictionaries for learners of English is built around a core vocabulary of 3,000 words – the so-called Oxford 3,000, although today the list is closer to 3,600 words – which are among the most useful and frequently occurring words in the language.

There are, of course, always outliers: the bard himself being just one such example. Shakespeare's written works make use of around 30,000 words.[71] And his passive or latent vocabulary – words that Shakespeare recognised, but didn't himself use in his works – has been estimated to amount to a further 35,000 words (this can be predicted, as passive vocabulary is usually at least double that of someone's active vocabulary). This provides a total vocabulary of around 65,000 words.[72] According to English language and Shakespeare expert David Crystal, the entire English vocabulary of the Elizabethan period was around 150,000 words. This means that Shakespeare had a vocabulary size that encompassed well over 40 per cent of the language.[73] In contrast, and assuming that today's English vocabulary, very conservatively, amounts to half a million words, the average contemporary man or woman has knowledge of a meagre 6 per cent of today's language.

The words of a language are divided into different lexical classes. For instance, in English, these include the so-called big four – nouns, verbs, adjectives and adverbs – that perform recognisably distinct semantic functions. Nouns range from the concrete – *table, tree, apple* – to the more abstract – *love, peace, explosion* – and tend to relate to thing-like entities, whether a person, place, object, event or idea. Verbs typically signal a process, something that continues over time. Processes can be actions that evolve over time (such as *to dance*), states that persist over time (like *to sleep*), or punctual events (like *to sneeze*), among others. An adjective most saliently relates to properties of nouns, with examples like *lacy* as in *lacy knickers*, or *bald* as in *bald head*. And finally, adverbs prototypically describe properties of verbs, such as *quickly*: *she walked quickly through the crowd*.

But this only scratches the surface. Other lexical classes in English include conjunctions, like *and, but* and *or*; prepositions such as *in, over, next to* and *in front of*; demonstratives such as *this* and *that*; and modal markers, historically derived from verbs, which express some kind of mental state ranging from intention to permission to obligation (such as *will, would, can, could, may, might, must, shall* and *should*). English even has words that, remarkably, can only appear in a single fixed expression, like *kith*, which today appears nowhere else in the language apart from the following: *kith and kin*.

All of these words are free-standing. But there is a class of linguistic units that cannot stand alone in this way. These include prefixes and suffixes that change the meaning of the word, for instance, *un-* and *-less*: *uninteresting* is not the same as *interesting*, and *hopeless* is not the same as *hope*. Other linguistic units that attach themselves to words include English inflections that can change the point in time when an event or action occurred, such as the past tense marker *-ed*: *kiss* versus *kissed*; and the plural marker *-s*: *lover* versus *lovers*. Finally, in this category we can include linguistically abbreviated elements like *-'ll*, as in *I'll go home*, or *-'m*, as in *I'm hungry*, linguistic units that are especially ubiquitous in spoken language.

But in addition, vocabulary items include those that are more complex. One kind includes the many thousands of idioms – fixed expressions whose meaning cannot be predicted from the individual words themselves – that a native speaker has at their disposal. Examples range from complex verbs – *to put in, to trip up* and *to run over something* – to stock phrases – *get your point across* – to popular phrases – *do or die, in it to win it* – and the many thousands of idiomatic expressions that a competent speaker of a language must just know: *answer the door, sound asleep, wide awake, all of a sudden, I can do that standing on my head, you could have knocked me over with a feather*.

The defining feature of a linguistic unit – whether a word, a unit that attaches itself to a word, or an idiom – is that it consists of a particular physical form: the spoken, signed or typed symbol that makes it up.

For instance, if I type the expression *wide awake* this is a specific physical representation that you can interact with and read on a page or a computer screen. But in addition, this physical representation has a particular conventional meaning associated with it. In the case of *wide awake*, English speakers all agree that the expression means a full state of wakefulness, rather than, say, a measurement of how long you've been awake for.

So, how does Emoji fare here? In contrast to English, Emoji has a far, far smaller 'vocabulary'. For instance, in Unicode version 9.0, released on 21 June 2016, seventy-two new emojis became available, bringing the total number of emojis to 1,815. But while new emojis are introduced each year, with each Unicode version update, the number of emojis available is vanishingly small compared to the range and complexity of vocabulary items that a competent native speaker possesses. A two-year-old may know as many as 300 words, while by the age of five, a child already possesses around 5,000 English words, reaching 12,000 by early teens – far outstripping the total number of emojis available.

One obvious reason for requiring a relatively large vocabulary is to provide a wide semantic range of expression. And here Emoji is highly impoverished compared to a natural language. Emoji fares well in terms of facial expressions (e.g. 'the lying face' emoji), hand gestures (e.g. the 'call me' emoji), animals (e.g. gorilla), food (e.g. bacon), as well as people (e.g. pregnant woman), sports (e.g. ice skating) and venues of holy worship (e.g. mosque). But it fares less well in terms of expressing more abstract ideas. Think about it: we have words, but no emojis, for: 'chaos', 'betrayal', 'social norm', 'duty', 'pithy' and 'empathy'. How these ideas might be captured by emojis is less clear.

Moreover, while it's possible to use emojis to express relatively simple ideas, such as a car, it's less clear how an emoji might express a more complex idea such as 'the beauty of the lines of a sports car', as experienced by petrol-head aficionados. But in this case, the difficulty is less the lack of emojis – compared to the number of words available in a language – but the sheer difficulty of expressing abstract ideas using a pictographic form; how would you go about representing, say, 'chauvinism', 'feminist', 'ethical' or 'iconoclastic' in Emoji? Emojis are pictographic in nature; one consequence is that they use images of things to represent the ideas they convey. But as many ideas are less tied to physical things, this provides a natural limit to what emojis can readily convey. Hence, Emoji is necessarily limited, up front, in terms of its semantic range. In contrast, this is where a language excels: it can express both concrete and far more abstract ideas with relative ease.

Let's now turn to the second organisational principle of language: its grammar. A grammatical system is a means of combining vocabulary items to create words and sentences of potentially great complexity. Word-formation processes assist us to build complex words in a range of ways. For instance, prefixes and suffixes can be added, as when we create complex words such as *anti-dis-establish-ment-arian-ism*. Words themselves can be combined to form compound words: *boathouse* versus *houseboat*. This process is rule-governed: a boathouse is a house (for boats), while a houseboat is a boat (that you live on). In English, the right-most element tells us what the newly coined word amounts to.

Furthermore, any given language is subject to language-specific principles that underpin the way in which words can be combined. For instance, some languages, such as English, make use of word order to provide the central organising principle of its grammar. Other languages eschew word order by using case: the means of indicating which words go together by using, for instance, suffixes on the words. A good example is classical Latin. Let's take the famous line from Virgil's *Eclogues* – here's the word-for-word translation:

Ultima	*Cumaei*	*venit*	*iam*	*carminis*	*aetas*
Last	Cumean	(is) come	now	song	age

The English translation would be: 'The last age of the Cumean song is now come'. But in the Latin, *ultima* ('last') and *aetas* ('age') are positioned either side of the verb *venit*, as are *Cumaei* ('Cumean') and *carminis* ('song'). And this is possible because 'last age' and 'Cumean song' are marked with suffixes that show they belong together – a suffix being a grammatical marker, much like the plural marker -*s* in English that is added to a noun to distinguish the plural *girls* from the singular *girl*.

In Latin, for instance, a noun has a stem with different variants – traditionally known as declensions – which would have allowed Latin speakers to recognise whether or not the word was the subject of the sentence. The various declensions of *aetas* are given in table below. Because an adjective, such as *ultimus* ('last'), would also have been declined to signal case, the upshot was this: Latin speakers in the time of Virgil would have recognised that both *ultima* and *aetas* were declined, to signal nominative case. Together they amount to the subject of the sentence. To make matters slightly more complicated, there were five types of Latin declension, corresponding to five broad types of word stem. It is for this reason that the word endings for *ultimus* and *aetas* are declined in slightly different ways, as *ultima* and *aetas* in Virgil's sentence. Nevertheless, Latin speakers would have known that these words go together, even though they are sequenced at opposite ends of the sentence.

	Case	Declension
1	Nominative	aetas
2	Genitive	aetatis
3	Dative	aetati
4	Accusative	aetaem
5	Ablative	aetate
6	Vocative	aetas

Declensions of the singular form of the Latin word for 'age'.

And if you thought grammatical case is an odd way of doing things, many languages spoken today do just this, from German to Romanian. In this way, words need not be arranged in a particular sequence in order to make sense. In modern English, which has lost much of the case system it possessed at an earlier point in its history, this is not possible.

Even those languages that use word order exhibit great variation. While we might naively assume that all languages use patterns like English, with the orthodox sentence beginning with a subject, followed by a verb and then a direct object – as in: *The rockstar smashed the guitar* – languages vary even here. For instance, the indigenous Australian language Jiwarli would convey the English sentence *This rockstar smashed that red guitar*, suitably translated, using the following word order: *That this red smashed rockstar guitar*.

So how does Emoji fare in the realm of grammar? One way of approaching this issue is to consider cases where digital communication is enacted entirely through the medium of emojis, without any text at all. One example of this, of course, is the case of Osiris Aristy that I discussed in the previous chapter. To interpret his police officer and handgun emojis as, collectively, conveying an intentional threat, as the New York District Attorney did, they had to be interpreted as conveying a compositional meaning. And this is what grammar does. Of course, there's far more to a natural language grammar than simply placing items alongside each other. After all, when items are adjacent to one another this implies a relationship in almost any domain: if two people stand closer together and apart from others in a crowd, we might infer that they are friends or lovers. Indeed, the principle of inferring that two or more entities are related by virtue of being close to one another is fundamental to how we see the world around us. It was first discovered, in the early twentieth century, by German psychologists who showed that this so-called gestalt or grouping principle of proximity is central to visual perception. Thus, interpreting a relationship between emojis that appear next to each other hardly counts as some kind of 'Emoji grammar'.

The hallmark of grammar, being able to combine words either

through word order (as in English) or through case (as in Latin), is, nevertheless, emerging in Emoji. While there are currently a little under 2,000 emojis, many of these are actually composite emojis: a sequence of emojis that come together in a single glyph. In such cases, while you or I might think we are selecting a unique emoji, in fact our computing operating system is selecting individual emojis, which are joined together, behind the scenes, with the equivalent of digital glue to look and act like a single emoji. The glue that performs the magic is the 'zero width joiner', or ZWJ for short. This blends the separate emojis together so that they form a single glyph. For instance, the female singer with dark brown skin is made up of three distinct emojis (see Figure 10 in the picture section) – the female emoji, the dark skin tone modifier and the microphone emoji.

But while the female singer and many others are made possible by Emoji grammar, this remains largely hidden from view, unless something goes wrong. To all intents and purposes, neither you nor I need to know the Unicode code points for a given emoji, nor how to combine them using a ZWJ in order to produce the female singer. On my smartphone, I simply select the female singer emoji – the software does everything else. It's only on a platform such as Twitter, where the number of characters are restricted, that you might notice that your female singer counts as three characters! And on platforms that don't support a particular 'compound' emoji, what you see might be just the female and microphone emojis, next to each other – here the hidden Emoji grammar unravels.

But of course, this emerging Emoji grammar is some considerable way from a true grammar. My lack of know-how means that, in effect, while I might know how to use and send emojis, I don't know how to combine them in a way that is grammatical. Without the smartphone in my pocket – which has more raw computing power than the computers of an entire nation from 1970 – I am a grammatical ignoramus (at least in the realm of joined-up emojis).

Symbols, symbols, symbols

Telepathy is a staple of science fiction, with many superheroes and villains possessing the ability to read someone else's thoughts; one of the most well-known examples is the Vulcan mind meld, a speciality of *Star Trek*'s Mr Spock. The term *telepathy* was coined in 1882 by Frederic W.H. Myers, the founder of the Society for Psychical Research. But in real life, telepathy is beyond the scope of ordinary mortals, and probably wouldn't be desirable anyway. As the popular aphorism has it: what other people think of you is none of your business, and knowing what others think would, most likely, do more harm than good.

In the absence of telepathy, humans use symbols that enable communication. As we saw in the previous chapter, a symbol is a physical representation that is conventionally attached to a meaning. But as systems of communication, language and Emoji make use of quite different sorts of symbol. And as we shall see, this helps explain why the semantic range of Emoji is relatively limited, compared to the seemingly limitless range of abstract thought that language helps us express.

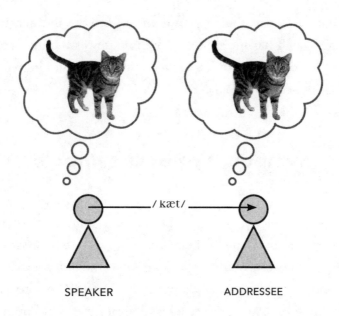

SPEAKER   ADDRESSEE

How linguistic communication conveys an idea.

Let's begin with language. In Chapter 2, we saw that the English word *cat*, made up of three sound segments, lets the speaker convey an idea, allowing the addressee to conjure up a mental idea (illustrated above).

So here's a question you may not have considered before: why, in English, do we use the symbol *cat*? After all, there is no causal relationship between the symbol – the word *cat* – and the idea it calls to mind. The English symbol, pronounced as /kæt/, doesn't look or sound like the entity it represents. In principle, any symbol would do – as long as it's not already in use in the language to convey a different idea. After all, different languages make use of very different symbols to evoke the same idea. For instance, the English *cat* is conveyed as *mace* in Albanian, *yata* in Greek, *kucing* in Maltese and *kissa* in Finnish. In short, the relationship between the symbol and the idea called to mind is completely arbitrary. The advantage of this, for a communicative system such as language, is that it makes possible great flexibility in communicative expression, as a symbol doesn't have to be connected, in the here and now, to the thing it stands for. There is nothing about the word *cat*, for instance, that looks or sounds like the idea it represents: a four-legged animal with whiskers and a tail that says miaow.

To show you what I mean, now let's consider the case of symbols that are causally related to the idea they call to mind. A key example of symbols of this kind are icons. Icons work by resembling the entity that they refer to – there is often a direct causal relationship between the icon and the idea it calls up. Take the desktop on your computer. The desktop interface lets us communicate with our computers. It does so by exploiting aspects of our everyday experience of interacting in the context of conventional office spaces. It achieves this by employing iconic reference. For instance, in a conventional office we have wastepaper baskets and recycling bins for disposing of unwanted letters, files, documents and other items. In the computer desktop interface, visual images serve as iconic representations that call to mind exactly these sorts of features of an ordinary office. An image of a recycling bin provides a useful mnemonic – an icon – based on something it resembles in a real office. Similarly, in the computer desktop interface, by dragging an icon for a file to the recycling bin icon, we succeed in having our computer delete the unwanted file.

So, while a natural language consists of symbols motivated by arbitrary convention – you just have to know that English speakers all agree to use the symbol *cat* to refer to the domestic pet of choice for many Western households – other communicative systems rely primarily on symbols that are iconic in nature.

How does Emoji line up on this score? On the whole, emojis are most typically icons – there is often a direct causal relationship between the glyph and the idea it calls up – in contrast to a linguistic symbol (where, as we know, the relationship is arbitrary). The smiley or winking faces look, more or less, like the ideas that they attempt to convey. Like the recycling bin on your computer desktop, they resemble the things they stand for. A smiley face or the poo emoji is forever tied to the thing it resembles. The table below compares and contrasts symbols in language versus Emoji.

Symbol type	Motivation	Example	Symptom of ...
Sign	Arbitrary	/kæt/ ('cat')	... a linguistic system (e.g. English)
Icon	Resemblance		... a non-linguistic system (e.g. Emoji)

Linguistic signs compared to Emoji icons.

We are now in a position to see why Emoji is less adept than language at representing abstract ideas. While a causal relationship between idea and glyph works just fine when representing concrete ideas, the situation becomes slightly trickier with the more abstract. After all, while a smiley can represent a smile, more abstract ideas have less obvious symbols that can be used to represent them. In a language the problem doesn't arise, as linguistic signs are abstract anyway: the English word *chaos* – which is a sign – refers to an abstract idea. But without a ready icon that can be used to represent the idea, it is less clear how we might capture the same notion with an emoji.

But while emojis are often icons, and words (in a language) are often abstract signs, the distinction is not always so clear-cut. Firstly, the distinction between linguistic symbols and icons is not as straightforward as we may think. For instance, English also makes use of iconic reference, on occasion, when calling things to mind. There is a class of words – onomatopoeias – that are essentially iconic in nature. The term *onomatopoeia* derives from the ancient Greek meaning 'echo or sound'. Onomatopoeias resemble the sounds produced; for example, we refer to the sound made by a bee as *buzzing*. The verb *to buzz* echoes the actual sound produced by bees: the linguistic symbol is in fact an icon. Hence, such words are linguistic icons. Iconic words of this sort are not restricted to animal sounds. The table below provides some examples of onomatopoeias in English.

Furthermore, using icons is not something unique to English. Other languages do it too. Corresponding onomatopoeias for animal sounds in French are presented in the next table. One point that's interesting, however, is that the divergence illustrates how two languages pick up on different aspects of a sound to provide quite different linguistic representations.

Type of sound	Onomatopoeias
Human vocal sounds	achoo, babbling, gargle, hiccup, hum, etc.
Human actions	smack, thump, etc.
Physical contact, movement or combustion	splat, boom, fizz, plop, whiz, slosh, swish, etc.
Sounds produced by devices	beep, ding ding, tick tock, vroom, zap, zip, etc.
Things named after the sounds they produce	choo choo (train), flip-flops, etc.
Animal names	cuckoo, dodo, etc.
Animal sounds	bleat, buzz, chirp, hiss, hoot, miaow, moo, purr, quack, ribbit, woof, etc.

Some examples of onomatopoeias in English.

Now let's turn to Emoji. Perhaps self-evidently, the range of happy, sad and winking faces are most clearly iconic. And this extends to emojis that relate to other semantic fields. For instance, there is a class of emojis that concern different countries, with the emoji for a specific country being represented by its flag. While this is iconic, the relationship between the communicative intention – the specific country – and a flag is less direct, iconically speaking, than a smiling face.

Think about it. A flag is an emblem, meant to represent a political entity, such as when the Union Flag represents the United Kingdom, or the Stars and Stripes the United States. A flag serves as an emblematic

Animal	English	French
Cat	miaow, purr	miaou, ron-ron
Dog	woof	ouah
Cockerel	cock-a-doodle-doo	cocorico
Songbird	tweet-tweet	cui-cui
Sheep	baa	bêêê
Donkey	ee-aw	hee-han
Frog	ribbit	coââ-coââ
Pig	oink-oink	groin-groin
Hen	cluck-cluck	cot-cot
Duck	quack-quack	coin-coin

Onomatopoeias for animal sounds in English and French.

proxy for the country it's representing. The emblem doesn't, itself, look like the country that it represents.

Another example along these lines is the clapping hands emoji. This iconically represents applause – especially when repeated, making a sequence of clapping-hand emojis. But of course, the communicative intention is to congratulate, especially in the context of a live performance of some kind. Here, not only is the meaning of the emoji not tied to the context of a live performance (from which the icon is derived), the clapping hands are meant to represent congratulations rather than merely two hands being banged together. So, the emoji functions as a generic means of signalling congratulations, despite being iconically motivated by contexts of live performance.

Another way of thinking about this is that the clapping-hands emoji derives from a specific cultural context: that involving acknowledging and praising a performance in a live musical or theatrical context. And this cultural basis for an emoji illustrates a further way in which the iconic basis for an emoji can be less directly motivated, becoming more symbolic and less iconic in the process.

Take an even clearer example: the two hands pressed together emoji. It was originally developed in the earliest Japanese Emoji system to convey the idea of please or thank you. But to Westerners, who don't have ready access to this cultural context, the emoji is generally taken to signal prayer or praying, and is often used to express the hope or aspiration for something to come to pass.

This illustrates two things. Firstly, the iconic basis for an emoji can be a matter of cultural difference: two hands folded or pressed firmly together, in Japanese culture, is directly motivated by the physical gesture made among the Japanese to convey *please* or *thank you*. But in Western cultures, this iconic motivation is less readily available; European and American cultures don't usually press their hands together to signal thanks. And secondly, the use by Westerners of the two hands pressed together emoji does not always iconically represent prayer, per se. Rather, it is often used to convey an aspiration or hope for something to come to pass.

The act of prayer among Christians, for instance, is often motivated by a desire to solicit divine intervention for a particular outcome: a loved one to recover rude health after grave illness, for instance, or to solicit forgiveness (from God, or indeed someone else), following some perceived transgression. The consequence is that the symbol associated with religious prayer – two hands pressed together – becomes associated not merely with the enactment of prayer, but with the aspirational focus, the motivation, of and for prayer in the first place. Hence, while the emoji can indeed be employed iconically, to signal the act of prayer, it can also be used to signal an aspiration or hope for something. And here, the direct iconic motivation is weakened. The emoji is being used symbolically, as a conventional means of representing a hope or aspiration. What all this shows is that emojis often veer towards symbolic dimensions of representation; the link between the glyph and how it is used is not always straightforwardly iconic.

What's more, the motivation for how an emoji looks can, on occasion, be entirely symbolic, just as is typically the case with spoken language. A particularly striking example of this can be seen with the three wise monkey emojis (shown below). In 2016, Twitter comedian Jonny Sun (@jonnysun),[74] alter-ego of Jonathan Sun, a researcher at MIT, asked users to decide whether there was just one wise monkey – who adopted three different poses – or three distinct monkeys, each one sporting a distinct pose.[75] His poll received over 211,000 votes, and Twitter users weighed in with their comments, including an intervention from one notorious Twitter user, @realDonaldTrump, the forty-fifth President of the United States (who came down on the side of three separate monkeys, dismissing those with the opposing viewpoint in characteristically forthright terms).[76] For the curious, the poll results scored a narrow victory for there being one monkey (53 per cent), versus three separate monkeys (47 per cent).

The three wise monkeys – they are, in fact, coded as three distinct emojis by Unicode – depict a pictorial maxim: see no evil, hear no evil, speak no evil. In Western tradition it is typically interpreted as advice not to turn a blind eye to inappropriate behaviour or conduct. In fact, this maxim derives from Japanese tradition, motivated by the teachings of Confucius, whose sayings include the following: 'Look not at what is contrary to propriety; listen not to what is contrary to propriety; speak not what is contrary to propriety.'[77]

The three wise monkey emoji – or is it emojis? [78]

The pictorial representation of the homily probably derives from a seventeenth-century woodcarving at Tōshō-gū shrine in Nikkō, Japan. The carving, which features Japanese macaque monkeys, a species common in Japan, uses the animal to represent the human life journey. But while this is a visual metaphor – holding the hands over the eyes, for instance, stands for not being able to see – the point is that there is nothing about three Japanese macaques, with their hands over various parts of their physiognomies, that iconically resembles the meaning of the maxim. You and I just have to know that the image relates to a particular idea. This is primarily an abstract representation, much like a linguistic sign:

the meaning conveyed by the image is motivated, only very indirectly, by an iconic relationship.

A final point here is that some linguistic systems function perfectly effectively – just like Emoji – in being largely iconic in nature. As already noted, sign languages are the functional equals of spoken language. But much of the motivation for signs in sign language is ultimately iconic rather that symbolic in nature. For instance, the American Sign Language symbols for 'cheerful', 'happy' and 'excited' all make use of an upward motion. And many linguists believe that positive states are iconically motivated by the human experience of being more upright, when feeling positive: *He was feeling on top of the world*; while negative experiences are iconically motivated by a lower posture: *She's down in the dumps*.[79]

Will Emoji evolve into a language?

Since the advent of Emoji on the global stage in 2011, I have often been asked whether it will evolve into a fully fledged language. In principle, it is possible to use a visual-textual system for language – the linguistic mode of communication is not something that is restricted to a particular medium of production; we will see an example of a visual language later in the book, in Chapter 6. But while Emoji exhibits impoverished expressiveness compared to language due to its limited range of symbols, what really lets it down is the lack of a grammar system.

But, in principle, it is possible to imbue Emoji with its own grammar system. Some aficionados have gone to great lengths to do exactly this. For instance, in Chapter 1, I briefly discussed the work of visual designer Ken Hale who has translated literary classics such as *Alice in Wonderland* and *Peter Pan* into Emoji. Consider one of the most famous lines from *Peter Pan*. Hale's emojified rendering is illustrated in Figure 11 in the picture section.

Hale created an Emoji grammatical system. He dubs his approach to creating an Emoji language as 'crypto-semantics'. Nevertheless, like any language, unless one goes through a process of learning what the symbols mean and how they are combined, then Hale's Emoji language remains for me, like you, a foreign tongue.

Unless there is value in the effort involved in creating and using a new grammatical system, it won't catch on. At present, Emoji functions not to replace the linguistic mode, but to complement it – the good old-fashioned English word is not going to be in danger any time soon. Emoji enables, arguably for the first time, a multimodal component to text-based digital communication, providing a code that fills out the communicative message in the linguistic mode, conveyed through text.

While learning Hale's Emoji language may be a step too far for some, there is simply no arguing with the expressive power of Emoji. Digital communication is the sign of our times. And Emoji functions extremely well in that medium, often in language-like ways. For this reason, it is surely not a stretch to consider an emoji to be, if not a word in the conventional sense, at the very least having language-like properties.

In the final analysis, asking whether Emoji may or will evolve into a language misunderstands both the function and significance of Emoji – to which we will return in the next chapter. Emoji, as a communicative system, a code, enables us to provide the non-verbal cues otherwise missing from textspeak. And this is a significant advance in our communicative wherewithal in the digital age. While Emoji will surely continue to evolve, and other systems and codes will be developed that will complement and, doubtless, replace Emoji as it currently exists, its emergence provides the beginning of a more or less level playing field, between face-to-face interaction and digital communication – better enabling effective communication in the digital sphere.

4

Emotionally Speaking

In the American TV crime drama *Lie to Me*, the British actor Tim Roth plays Dr Cal Lightman, a world-leading authority on facial expressions. Lightman and his team accept assignments from federal and local law-enforcement agencies that require their expertise; Lightman and his associates are second to none in detecting whether a suspect is lying during interrogation, by studying their facial expressions and body language and what these reveal about their emotions.

The TV series is based on a branch of applied psychology, made famous by the American forensic psychologist Professor Paul Ekman, dubbed the 'best human lie detector in the world'.[80] Ekman pioneered the study of emotional expression by developing a technique for studying micro-expressions – fleeting facial features. There are over 10,000 of them, produced by up to forty-three facial muscles when we experience joy, anger, sadness, guilt and disgust.[81] Ekman developed a facial coding system that allows videotaped interviews to be analysed by sophisticated software systems. The system uses the geometrical features of a subject's face in order to help detect whether they are telling the truth or not. This expertise led to Ekman becoming one of the twentieth century's most widely cited psychologists. His prowess also ensured that those with a vested interest in deciphering emotions from facial expression beat a path to his door – Ekman has worked as a consultant to police departments, anti-terrorism agencies, as well as the *Lie to Me* production team.

If the eyes are the window to the soul, then the face is a barometer of our emotional selves. Nowhere is this clearer, perhaps, than with the forty-fifth President of the United States, Donald Trump, whose facial expressions, not to mention explosive tweets, often reveal how he feels on a given subject. In an analysis commissioned by the *Guardian*, psychologist Peter Collett examined the seven signature facial expressions of Donald Trump, providing insight into the president's emotional self.[82] From the alpha face, to the chin-jut, to the zipped smile, Trump's face broadcasts how he feels, and what he wants us to think and feel along with him.

So how does this relate to digital communication? Research conducted by Kristin Byron of Syracuse University, in the United States, examined how we interpret emotion in emails – over 100 billion are sent and received on a daily basis. It was found that the lack of non-verbal cues, such as facial and bodily expression, means addressees are not very good at interpreting the emotional expression of the sender.[83] No matter how carefully we might try to craft our message, we are prone to the 'not so smiley-face of email confusion', as one report dubbed the finding.[84]

This adds up to what I call the angry jerk phenomenon: in everyday electronic communication, many of us have experienced the email or digital text that reads as if the person at the other end of the message is plain hopping mad. One of the problems, of course, with digital communication such as email is that it sucks away any vestiges of empathy. In real-life contexts, using spoken language, we can interpret what our addressee intends to convey, via language, through non-verbal cues: their posture, gaze, facial expressions and gestures. We also have speech prosody to guide us, such as the rise and fall of spoken pitch contours that, most saliently perhaps, signal whether something is a statement or a question. What's more, we can adjust what we're saying and, perhaps more importantly, how we're saying it, from our addressee's responses, verbal and non-verbal. We use these social cues to adjust, during the ebb and flow of ongoing talk, what we're conveying in order to clearly signal our intentions – what we wish our addressee to take away with them.

But in the realm of digital speak, once we've pressed the send button, we no longer have control of the message, and how it is interpreted. And when we receive a message, all the non-verbal cues are missing; not only do we have no way of knowing whether the message was sent by someone in red-faced anger, or blissfully sipping a Martini on a beach somewhere – all the nuancing has evaporated. Too often, someone who we know to be otherwise calm and sane can come across as an angry twerp. This is where Emoji comes in. Without recourse to facial expression, Emoji assists us to communicate emotion more effectively, avoiding miscommunication and causing offence.

Communicating empathy

First impressions matter. When we meet someone new, we seldom remain neutral: good or bad, we form an immediate opinion of them – too brash, too boring, engaging, drab, shy, and so it goes. This is, in large part, based on non-verbal cues – their appearance, their body language, their mannerisms – rather than what they say. We use these cues to form an emotional response that informs the way we view the other person. And we do all this in just a tenth of a second![85]

In some contexts, first impressions are of the utmost importance, as when chatting with a prospective date – who might, eventually, become your life partner (or not, as the case may be). As for the dreaded job interview, sage advice invariably counsels that we come across well from the outset, that hiring decisions are often decided within the first few minutes.

This is more than mere folk wisdom: it's backed up by scientific research. In one leading study, researchers examined hiring decisions based on a survey of 600 thirty-minute interviews. They found that around 5 per cent of decisions, whether to hire or not, were made in the first minute; around a quarter of decisions in the first five minutes; and a whopping 60 per cent within the first fifteen minutes. Before an interview is even halfway through, and before you've managed to get to grips with those butterflies in your stomach, your fate is already sealed.[86]

In our everyday encounters, how we respond to others is, in large part, determined by how we respond to them emotionally. We give up our seat on the bus or the train because we recognise and empathise with the greater need of others – the elderly, disabled, or the clearly exhausted mother-to-be. We respond positively, in a humdrum service encounter, to the employee with the winning smile and polite turn of phrase, and negatively to the ill-mannered youth who bumps past us in the street. Empathy is a key factor in understanding others, and a central ingredient in deriving meaning from social interactions. And this appears to arise, in large measure, from the non-verbal cues that abound in our everyday social encounters.

While empathy, in its most rudimentary form, is often understood as an awareness of the feelings and emotions of others, it involves more than this. According to a leading expert on emotional intelligence, empathy is an 'awareness of others' feelings, needs and concerns', and requires 'sensing others' feelings and perspectives, and taking an active interest in their concerns'.[87] Oxford Dictionaries defines empathy as: 'The ability to understand and share the feelings of another.'[88] So how do we form our experiences of others? How do we actually 'experience' the experiences of others, in order to demonstrate a sensitivity to and, indeed, an active interest in their concerns? How do we get to stand in their shoes, so to speak, to get to grips with what they are about, and more importantly, what they mean, in everyday communication?

Verbal cues – the words we string together in spoken utterances – are only part of the story. Of course, it stands to reason that in certain contexts, what others say, using language, is the key ingredient in meaning-making: in a public lecture, for instance, the message is largely conveyed by the words. Sure, we can gain a lot of information from the speaker's body language; but the content, the message, is right there in the words they've chosen for their talk. Yet, in our daily face-to-face interactions with strangers, family members, work colleagues and friends, we respond to a far greater degree to non-verbal information.

On one estimate, only 30–35 per cent of the social dimensions of meaning – such as our emotional expression, our personality and how we relate to others – come from language; in our daily interactions with others, up to a staggering 70 per cent may derive from non-verbal cues.[89] This includes the visual cues such as the other person's body language, facial expression and gestures, as well as how close they stand to us – we've all experienced the discomfort of the individual who occupies too much of our personal space; our emotional response is likely to be negative. We also respond to their physical appearance, their dress, as well as the environment in which we encounter them, which provides information about their occupation or lifestyle. We also draw information from touch – I once knew a successful businessman who claimed to be able to tell how reliable a potential partner or client was from how they shook his hand. But is there any truth to this anecdote?

According to research, there really is: the strength of our handshake gives away telltale signs about our personality. In one of the first studies of its kind, researchers investigated the relationship between handshake strength and personality.[90] In the study, 112 subjects shook hands with four trained coders – twice with each coder – in order to assess grip strength of the handshake. The subjects also completed assessments of personality traits. The research found that a strong handshake, across both sexes, correlates with being an extrovert and emotionally expressive. In contrast, a weak handshake tends to correlate with introversion and being less emotionally expressive.

We derive further information from observing self-touch: someone touching their hair might be bored, or perhaps signalling romantic interest. We also glean information from how others manage the ongoing, smooth flow of conversation (time between turns in an exchange), as well as eye contact, pupil dilation (especially in assessing the likelihood of a potential romantic encounter) and even blink rate.

All these dimensions of non-verbal communication were studied by the late American anthropologist Ray Birdwhistell, a pioneering figure in this area of research. He founded the field of kinesics, as he dubbed it, which involved the study of the role of 'facial expression, gestures, posture and gait, and visible arm and body movements' in conveying social meaning.[91] Viewed through this lens, it is perhaps no accident that Emoji, with its bewildering array of yellow faces, ranging from the assorted permutations on a smile through to the various confused, unamused, sad and angry faces, is so apt for visual communication in textspeak.

The other dimension of non-verbal communication involves paralinguistic features of speech, first studied by the American linguist Alfred Trager.[92] Paralinguistics is the study of the features that accompany spoken language, as a consequence of its medium of production, and which can influence and even alter the meaning of the words we utter. Paralinguistic features range from vocal signals, such as laughter, to speech prosody, which includes rhythm, relative volume, pitch, intonation and the pitch range the voice operates in – higher for women, on average, than men.

Prosody derives from the ancient Greek meaning 'song sung to music'. Spoken language has a musical quality associated with it. And this derives from the way it is produced via the articulators, such as the tongue, mouth, lips, and the vibrating folds in our voice box, as well as the musculature that we use to control the articulators. While the prosody of our own language can seem like music to our weary ears – especially after a prolonged absence abroad, struggling, disadvantaged and ill at ease with a foreign tongue you might mangle (at best) – the absence of prosody can lead to the perception of someone's speech being monotonous, perhaps even sinister. This is famously evidenced by the morally and emotionally ambiguous Professor Snape, played by the late, great Alan Rickman, in the Harry Potter movies.

For some, animating their spoken language seems a challenge – as a young student, I once had the misfortune to be taught by an otherwise erudite and knowledgeable professor who seemingly possessed the ability to send his students to sleep – watching paint dry would have been more entertaining. But in fact, there is a clinical condition that afflicts some people who are unable to correctly modulate their speech. This is known as aprosodia; it results in an impairment in properly varying pitch, loudness, rhythm and intonation – such as the rise and fall of speech contours – during speech. Sufferers not only sound flat and monotonous when they speak, they are also unable to convey emotion in spoken language or infer the emotions of others as conveyed during spoken interaction. Aprosodia is sometimes evident in people afflicted with Asperger's syndrome. This reveals just how essential prosody is to communication: it's one of the key ways in which we convey information that helps our addressee to empathise with us in spoken interaction. It provides a direct means of signalling our emotional stance and our attitude, as well as placing focus on specific parts of words, entire words and phrases.

All emotional

While our non-verbal cues, both kinesics and paralanguage (the features that accompany spoken language), contribute in important ways to social meaning in face-to-face communication, they fulfil different functions with regard to language itself. In landmark research in the 1960s and 1970s, the late British psychologist Michael Argyle claimed that while we use spoken language to convey information about events and states of affairs, non-verbal information, such as intonation, facial expression and gesture, is used to express communicative attitudes towards others, and, in part, to establish and maintain rapport in interpersonal interactions.[93] His best-selling books on the psychology of interpersonal behaviour[94] and bodily communication[95] remain classics, and made Argyle, an Oxford don, one of the best-known social psychologists of the twentieth century.

One reason for the expressive power of paralanguage and kinesics is that it is less embarrassing or risky to communicate emotional messages via non-verbal cues. Another is that we are less able to suppress our non-verbal emotional responses. Indeed, this was Darwin's observation in one of the earliest treatises on non-verbal communication: *The Expression of the Emotions in Man and Animals*, published in 1872. Many aspects of our body language, especially our display of primary emotions such as fear, anger, happiness and sadness – in facial expressions – are involuntary. And this means that the information we obtain from non-verbal communication can undercut what the words themselves say – the civil *Nice to see you*, uttered by your ex after a messy break-up, can be contorted by the gritted teeth, through which the apparent pleasantry is spat at you; this provides a truer tell of how she or he feels upon bumping into you. Non-verbal cues also persist when the words dry up: body language is continuous, persisting during the awkward silences, and providing a steady stream of information for us to read the other's true thoughts and feelings.

Specifically, we use non-verbal communicative cues to express our emotions, our attitudes towards our addressee and others, and towards the message being conveyed. We also use non-verbal cues to manage the flow of ongoing talk between speakers and addressees – such as when we have finished speaking, and wish to give up the 'floor'; we also use them to present our personality, and in cultural rituals such as greetings.[96] An obvious example of the latter is in the difference between so-called high-contact versus low-contact cultures: whether or not a culture is 'touchy-feely'. Compare the stereotype of the expressive warmth of Mediterranean Europeans or inhabitants of Latin America – lots of casual sleeve-touching, open-body postures, smiling and eye contact – with that of the reputed sangfroid of the British stiff upper lip, arguably best embodied by the dysfunctional, emotional frigidity of the James Bond novels and films.

In the field of psychology, there has been extensive research into just how much store we place in non-verbal communication, especially in the realm of communicating emotion. In early, famous research, the psychologist Albert Mehrabian compared the relative contribution of language, paralinguistic cues and body language in conveying social meaning.

In one study, subjects were asked to evaluate whether a speaker was being positive or negative when uttering specific words, such as *terrible* or *dear*.[97] Mehrabian examined two modes: the linguistic and the paralinguistic. Sometimes a negative word (e.g. *terrible*) was spoken using a positive tone of voice – for instance, higher pitch range and rising pitch – while a positive word (e.g. *dear*) was spoken using a negative pitch contour. Mehrabian found that in such cases, the paralinguistic cue trumped the linguistic mode. When the emotional expression in the paralinguistic mode diverged from the meaning of the word, subjects relied more on in the non-verbal cue.

In a second study, Mehrabian added a second type of non-verbal cue to the mix, namely facial expressions. In addition to hearing the positive or negative words, subjects were also shown photographs of people's faces, with positive (e.g. happy) versus negative (e.g. sad) expressions. He calculated the relative importance of kinesics versus paralinguistic cues, and found that subjects set relatively greater store in facial expressions than emotional expression due to tone of voice, by a ratio of 3:2.[98]

Based on these two sets of findings, Mehrabian used a formula to work out how much emotional meaning subjects were deriving from the three distinct modes: language, paralanguage and facial expression (a form of kinesics). He found that only 7 per cent of his subjects' emotional responses to others came from language – the literal meanings of the words they heard. In contrast, an impressive 38 per cent came from paralanguage, leaving over half, a whopping 55 per cent, to be derived from facial expression. Based on his data, Mehrabian found that when communicating emotional responses, over 90 per cent of what we derive comes not from what others say – from their words – but from how they say it, and what they do while they say it.

While Mehrabian's overall conclusion – what has come to be known as the '7 per cent-38 per cent-55 per cent rule' – strikingly illustrates the significance of the non-verbal aspects of social interaction in communication, caution is nevertheless in order. His research was focused on the way in which we express emotions, and the judgement others pass on us when we do so. Moreover, he used single words, which were tape-recorded; and his subjects were all female. His experiments, therefore, while pioneering, were far from complete.

Subsequent research found that when subjects are making a judgement about the person, rather than just their emotional expression, verbal communication becomes more important.[99] The verbal or linguistic mode also appears to be more important when someone is making an assessment as to whether another person is honest or deceptive.[100] And the more language there is – by which I mean the more content that is provided through language to adequately explain something, such as when recounting a complex food recipe, or when providing detailed instructions on how to build something – the more important verbal communication becomes.[101] Finally, the gender of the addressee and speaker affects the relative importance of the mode used for communication purposes, whether it be verbal or non-verbal.[102] Nevertheless, what this all reveals is that effective communication requires both verbal and non-verbal cues – and it's the non-verbal cues that appear to be especially geared towards facilitating emotional expression and inducing empathy.

Oh, the irony!

A case in point is irony – saying the opposite of what you mean. I am being ironic when I congratulate my marketing friend for an epic marketing fail (illustrated below) with the words: 'Hope is fifty yards ahead; great ad placement, mate.' And if I continue with the humiliation, 'You deserve a bonus!', I'm deploying a more specific kind of irony – sarcasm – where the irony is aimed at an individual, rather than a situation.[103]

Poor ad placement choice.[104]

While we use irony for humorous effect, we also deploy it to establish empathy. People respond better to criticism if it's delivered ironically, as this softens the blow. For instance, many of us have stories about inadvertent 'reply to all' email embarrassments. An acquaintance once sent an email 'reply to all', in response to a female co-worker's mass email notifying the company about her change of surname. His reply was 'Congratulations'. The only problem, however, was that the name change was due to divorce, not marriage; the co-worker was reverting to her maiden name. His faux pas drew an ironic response from his boss: 'Well judged there, buddy.'

The reason that irony works to soften criticism is because of its ability to tinge what is actually meant, with what is literally said. Saying 'well done' or 'great job' in response to poor work allows some of the positive sentiment of the words to rub off on the implied criticism. But this ability of irony works in both directions.[105] For this reason, a compliment can be downgraded if delivered ironically, as the irony tinges the implied positive sentiment with the negative words that are actually uttered. For instance, telling a record-breaking salesman, 'You're the worst ever!' reduces the effect of the compliment – and can even sound snide or envious.

In the realm of textspeak, without ready access to the non-verbal cues that we often draw upon to interpret irony, miscommunication is rife. An addressee might, without the empathy-inducing non-verbal cues, interpret an ironic expression literally or, vice versa, a literal expression ironically. And this can lead to inadvertently getting your addressee's back up. But here, again, Emoji can help.

Recent research has shown that using visual representations of faces, notably the wink and the joking face (with one eye closed and the tongue sticking out), which are the most commonly used emojis to signal irony, can help avoid miscommunication in textspeak.[106] In a study at Nottingham University, in England, 192 students were given text messages to read.[107] For some of the messages, context was provided: 'Tanya had noticed that Jenny had put on a lot of weight', making it clear that the ensuing message, from Tanya to Jenny, was meant sarcastically: 'I see the diet is going well.' In others, there was no context, resulting in a message that was ambiguous between literal versus sarcastic interpretations. Participants were then asked to judge whether a sarcastic or literal meaning was intended. While some subjects were shown messages without a sarcasm marker: a wink or a joking face emoticon – typographically produced faces were used, such as ;-) (wink) or :-p (tongue sticking out), rather than emojis – others *were* presented with sentences with emoticons signalling sarcasm. The results were very clear: without a sarcasm marker, ambiguous messages tended to be interpreted literally. But with sarcasm markers, ambiguous sentences were more likely to be taken as sarcastic.

In terms of avoiding miscommunication in textspeak, the conclusions are clear. As sarcasm has a tingeing effect, thereby flipping the sentiment of the words, emojis should be used with care. They can be used to help show, in textspeak, when you're being ironic. But if you want your words to stand at face value, to literally praise or criticise, emojis are best avoided.

But this all leads to one final issue. Given the myriad ways in which we signal irony in the age of Emoji, which emoji is best? To find out, one intrepid writer, for the social media content company Crocstar, asked Twitter exactly this: 'Emoji-loving friends. Please tweet me the emojis you use when you want to show you're being sarcastic (it's for a blog post).'[108] Twitter duly responded. From the smirking face and the eye roll, to the unamused face, and the upside-down smile, Emoji enables carefully calibrated irony, providing a spectrum of sarcastic markers suitable for any occasion (see Figure 12 in the picture section).

The many faces of emotion

So much of our emotional expression comes directly from our facial expressions. But when online, and hampered by the lack of non-verbal cues in textspeak, Emoji comes into its own with its suite of yellow faces. The table below provides an extensive list.

😀	Grinning face	😅	Smiling face with open mouth and cold sweat
😁	Grinning face with smiling eyes	😆	Smiling face with open mouth and closed eyes
😂	Face with tears of joy	😉	Winking face
🤣	Rolling on the floor laughing	😊	Smiling face with smiling eyes
😃	Smiling face with open mouth	😋	Face savouring delicious food
😄	Smiling face with open mouth and smiling eyes	😎	Smiling face with sunglasses

	Smiling face with heart-eyes		Disappointed but relieved face
	Face blowing a kiss		Face with open mouth
	Kissing face		Zipper-mouth face
	Kissing face with smiling eyes		Hushed/surprised face
	Kissing face with closed eyes		Sleepy face
	Smiling face		Tired face
	Slightly smiling face		Sleeping face
	Hugging face		Relieved face
	Thinking face		Nerd face
	Neutral face		Face with stuck-out tongue
	Expressionless face		Face with stuck-out tongue and winking eye
	Face without mouth		Face with stuck-out tongue and closed eyes
	Face with rolling eyes		Drooling face
	Smirking face		Unamused face
	Persevering face		Face with cold sweat

	Pensive face		Anguished face
	Confused face		Fearful face
	Upside-down face		Weary/distraught face
	Money-mouth face		Grimacing face
	Astonished face		Face with open mouth and cold sweat
	Frowning face		Face screaming in fear
	Slightly frowning face		Flushed face
	Confounded face		Dizzy face
	Disappointed face		Angry face
	Worried face		Lying face
	Face with steam from nose		Face with thermometer
	Crying face		Nauseated face
	Loudly crying face		Sneezing face
	Frowning face with open mouth		Smiling face with horns

The many faces of emotion.[109]

In one study, conducted by the software developer SwiftKey, Emoji usage was analysed in over 1 billion items of data, taken from across sixteen language groups. It found that nearly half of the Emoji usage from this sample related to yellow faces expressing positive emotional sentiment (including smiles, grins, winks and so on), while nearly 15 per cent related to faces expressing a negative emotional sentiment (sad and crying faces, etc.). In total, this means that around 60 per cent of total emoji usage involves faces expressing a range of positive and negative emotions (see Figure 13 in the picture section for more detail).

But while it seems that Emoji is an effective means of better enabling us to express our emotional selves in textspeak, not all emojis are created equal in their emotional resonance. A team of psychologists investigated how Twitter users deploy emojis to express their emotions.[110] To do this, they analysed over 1.6 billion tweets across thirteen different languages. Trained annotators – eighty-three in total – read each tweet and gave it an emotional value (positive, neutral or negative). Using sophisticated statistical techniques, the researchers drew on this data to produce a detailed 'Sentiment Ranking' for the 751 most commonly used emojis in the tweets. This has provided, for the first time, a detailed comparison of the emotional value we attach to a given emoji – based on what it means, and what it shows about the emotion being expressed in a particular tweet.

The table here gives the sentiment ranking for the top ten most frequent emojis in the Twitter sample used to calculate the rankings. The scale for calculating the sentiment is as follows: 1.0 is 100 per cent positive/happy; 0 is neutral; −1.0 is 100 per cent negative/sad. Hence, a score of 0.75 for the love heart emoji has a very high positive sentiment ranking.

Emoji	Number of occurances	Sentiment ranking	Description
	14,622	0.22	Face with tears of joy
	8,050	0.75	Red heart
	7,144	0.66	Heart suit
	6,359	0.68	Smiling face with heart eyes
	5,526	0.09	Loudly crying face
	3,648	0.70	Face blowing a kiss
	3,186	0.64	Smiling face with smiling eyes
	2,925	0.56	OK hand sign
	2,400	0.63	Two hearts
	2,336	0.52	Clapping hands

Sentiment rankings for the top ten most frequently used emojis on Twitter. [111]

The function of silent messages

In our everyday spoken interactions we sometimes send mixed messages. Telling someone that of course they haven't offended you, while avoiding eye contact and presenting closed body language, tells them that they very much have. In such scenarios, people tend to privilege the non-verbal cues over the words themselves: body language trumps the words they say.[112] Our silent messages are often the most powerful.

For communication to really succeed it must make use of different modes, typically at the same time, and avoid mixed messages: when body language and paralanguage are not aligned with what the words themselves are saying.

Take gesture: our gestures are minutely choreographed to co-occur with our spoken words. Not only do they nuance and complement our spoken words – a pointing finger makes it clear which pastry we have selected, while nothing offends quite like showing someone the finger, a gestured insult – we also seem unable to suppress them. Watch someone on the telephone; they'll be gesticulating away, despite their gestures being unseen by the person on the other end of the line. In lab settings when psychologists run experiments in which subjects are required to communicate without gesture, spoken language suffers; if gestures are suppressed, then our speech actually becomes less fluent.[113] We need to gesture to be able to speak properly. And, by some accounts, gesture may have even been the route that language took in its evolutionary emergence.

Eye contact is another powerful signal we use in our everyday encounters. We use it to manage our spoken interactions with others.

Speakers avert their gaze from an addressee when talking, but establish eye contact to signal the end of their utterance. We gaze at our addressee to solicit feedback, but avert our gaze when we disapprove of what they are saying. We also glance at our addressee to emphasise a point we're making.

Eye gaze, gesture, facial expression and speech prosody are powerful non-verbal cues that convey meaning; they let us express our emotional selves, as well as providing an effective and dynamic means of managing our interactions on a moment by moment basis. Face-to-face interaction is multimodal, with meaning conveyed in multiple, overlapping and complementary ways. This provides a rich communicative environment, with multiple cues for coordinating and managing our spoken interactions.

In essence, language, paralanguage and kinesics form a unified communicative signal. The suppression of one non-verbal cue, for instance gesture, impairs the spoken signal. Visual information achieved by kinesics, aural information conveyed by paralanguage, and linguistic information conveyed via (spoken) language are all required to fully realise the intended speaker's meaning conveyed by an utterance.[114]

It turns out that there are six main ways in which non-verbal cues enhance meaning in face-to-face spoken interaction.[115] The first is substitution. I can say *yes*; or, I can nod. Here we have a case where body language can straightforwardly replace a verbal expression. A clear case where non-verbal cues can replace language is a type of gesture known as an emblem. Examples include the OK sign, or the thumbs-up gesture. Emblematic gestures like these speak for themselves: they have a stable meaning, and are instantly recognisable without verbal support, in more or less the same way as an English word, such as *cat*, is instantly recognisable to other English speakers. Moreover, gestures of this kind may be culture specific. As we saw in the previous chapter, in Japanese culture two hands placed firmly together means *please* or *thank you*, while in Western culture this is a symbol of prayer.

On some occasions, however, we use two modes to say the same thing, facilitating the second function: reinforcement. I can both say *no*, and I can shake my head. Here the kinesic cue is repeating the verbal cue.

But sometimes using two modes simultaneously can be used to give a mixed message, the third function; and this can be both deliberate and have communicative value. For instance, the linguistic expression *This will be fun*, said with a monotone delivery and facial grimace, deploys paralinguistic and kinesic cues in order to contradict the verbal expression. But the function here is to create a humorous effect, by using non-verbal cues to prompt an ironic reading.

The fourth function, a particularly important one, of non-verbal cues is to complement the verbal expression: to add information not otherwise present in the spoken words. For instance, if someone is offered a glass of wine, they might respond, *Yes, please*, while using a gesture involving the thumb and forefinger parallel, just a couple of centimetres apart, to indicate just a small amount of wine. In this case, the gesture is providing supplementary information, indicating the amount of wine required, and otherwise not available from the spoken response. This complements and clarifies the information contained in the spoken utterance, helping out the addressee in the process.[116]

Many uses of speech prosody complement the linguistic mode,

sometimes even changing their meaning in the process. Here's an example I've sometimes used in media interviews to make this point. Take the utterance *I love you*. In standard American or British English, with falling pitch, the utterance is a declaration of undying love. But with rising pitch, said as a question, it becomes a derisive counterblast that can serve as an ironic put-down (and best not practised out loud, if you wish to keep your nearest as your dearest). In fact, *I love you*, with rising pitch, doesn't do what it says on the tin: it means the opposite of what it says.

Speech intonation also tells us about a speaker's attitudes and emotional responses – another example of the complementing function. A fall from high pitch on the first syllable of a word, for instance, can signal greater excitement, or warmth. Try experimenting by adjusting the pitch contour of *hello*. If you start with higher pitch on the 'hel' of *hello*, this is typically judged as warmer, as when greeting an old friend, than when starting from low pitch, when answering an annoying phone call, when engrossed in another task.

The fifth way in which non-verbal cues support verbal expression is to provide an emphasising or accenting function. With regard to kinesic cues, a common way this is achieved is the use of 'beat' gestures; these are gesticulations that provide simple, rhythmic motions, made with the hands or fingers. These add emphasis to what's being said, or express our emotional state. For instance, as psychologist Daniel Casasanto explains: '[f]ast staccato beats may show agitation; precise beats may show determination or sincerity; large, forceful beats may show either frustration or enthusiasm'.[117]

Paralinguistic cues also signal the relative importance of different parts of an utterance. For instance, falling pitch can be used to signal what is new information. The sentence *I saw a* ↘ *burglar* might answer the question *What did you see?* Here, falling pitch (signalled by the arrow) from the previous word onto *burglar* emphasises the answer – the new information.

Finally, non-verbal cues also play an important function in the management and flow of ongoing discourse. Let's start with gestures; for instance, the same gesture made at an earlier point in the conversation is repeated at a later point. And this works to tie the two points in the conversation together. We also use gestures when we can't find the word we're looking for, such as the finger placed against the lips to denote thinking.

Other sorts of kinesics can be used to regulate our communicative exchanges. Nodding and shaking the head, at appropriate places in a conversation, provides backchannel support, showing the other person that we are following and engaging with what they are saying, and that we agree and disagree. As noted earlier, eye gaze is also known to have an important regulatory function. Speakers avert their gaze from an addressee when talking, but establish eye contact to signal the end of their utterance.[118]

And of course, paralinguistic cues also play a ubiquitous role in managing the flow of our spoken interactions. For instance, intonation has an important function in regulating the way in which we interact with one another in conversation. In written text, we know where one word ends and another begins due to the white spaces between words. And punctuation conventions, like the comma, full stop, exclamation and question marks, signal how written sentences should be parsed, divided up and interpreted. Think about it for a second: in spoken language, there are no question marks; and there are no spaces between words. Instead, we have the melodic rise and fall of pitch contours, acceleration and deceleration of the speech tempo, the variation in loudness, the emphasis or stress placed on specific syllables, all of which collectively punctuate our spoken language.

Beyond the angry jerk phenomenon

So, how does Emoji enable emotional expression in textspeak? And how does it help us to induce an empathetic response in our addressee, avoiding the angry jerk phenomenon? The short answer is that Emoji is to textspeak what non-verbal cues are to spoken interaction. The primary function of Emoji, at least as it is currently used, is not to usurp language, but to provide the non-verbal cues essential to effective communication that are otherwise missing from textspeak. Emoji is to textspeak what kinesics and paralanguage are to spoken language, and fulfils exactly the same six functions that non-verbal cues do in face-to-face linguistic interaction.

We begin, firstly, with the substitution function. In textspeak, sometimes all that's required is an emoji: in response to an especially hilarious remark, say; on occasion, nothing more is required than the face with tears of joy emoji, which speaks volumes. And in the case of the Andy

Murray tweet in Chapter 1, emojis were all that was needed, substituting for language to describe the roller-coaster ride of a wedding day.

The reason why an emoji can substitute for text is because an individual emoji amounts to a visual gestalt. The term gestalt, which derives from the German, refers to perceiving the whole (and was the name given to an approach to perceptual psychology in the early part of the twentieth century; see Chapter 3).[119] An emoji is a gestalt in the sense that it encapsulates an often complex set of experiences in a single, intuitively accessible glyph. The face with tears of joy emoji is a fine example: it conveys a complex emotional spectrum in a single pictogram that is both instantly recognisable and which we can all relate to. In comparison, consider the number of words required to convey the same idea in English. But while emojis can substitute for words in our digital messages, a delicate hand is nevertheless required in how we choose to use Emoji. In discussing the etiquette of Emoji and dating, one twenty-something reports how the rush to use Emoji can be as bad for your dating prospects as turning up late, or talking about your ex on the first date:

A guy once asked me out with almost nothing but emoji, which was cute and all, but I was a little turned off because what would happen when we had to rely on words instead of characters? It was a tough call: I didn't want to ruin my chance with a fun-loving and carefree guy all over a couple of symbols, but his excessive use tore apart the first impression that I had had of him. He had rushed into the emoji relationship.[120]

Enough said!

Secondly, Emoji fulfils the reinforcement function. After all, one of the joys of an emoji is that it can be repeated, as when someone declares their love for you, followed by a line of love hearts. This provides a multimodal declaration of true love. In so doing, Emoji is also achieving an emphasising function. The more emojis there are, the more the message conveyed by the linguistic mode is reinforced: the more the declaration of love is truly, madly and deeply.

A case in point is the avid emoji-tweeting Julie Bishop, Australian Member of Parliament and Minister for Foreign Affairs, and arguably that country's most influential woman. We first met Ms Bishop in Chapter 1, in the context of Vladimir Putin as the angry, red-faced man emoji, from her emojified political interview. But Julie Bishop's Emoji usage often exemplifies a number of the main functions of Emoji. Take a pre-Christmas tweet (see Figure 14 in the picture section), sent on 4 December 2015. Much of the tweet includes emojis that reinforce the linguistic message. Clear examples include the emoji for post office, which is used to reinforce the use of parliament – the pictogram for a post office on Twitter has a dome that looks somewhat parliamentary – the thumbs-up and hand-clapping emojis are deployed to emphasise the gratitude expressed, and the use of star-themed emojis help highlight the idea of a stellar year.

But Julie Bishop's tweet also illustrates other functions of Emoji. For instance, she substitutes emojis for words to signal global plane travel and Christmas. And her final six emojis, which all relate to vacation activities, complement her holiday season good wishes at the end of the tweet – we will get to the complementing function of Emoji below.

Emoji can also be used to provide the third, contradictory, function. For instance, the rolling eyes emoji – the Emoji code's 'snarky grace note', as one commentator has so aptly dubbed it[121] – provides an excellent example.

Take a tweet posted by British sports anchor and celebrity Gary Lineker during the course of the Euro 2016 international soccer tournament. The tournament features leading international teams from across Europe. During the course of the tournament, England, a major soccer power, had been eliminated by lowly Iceland. In the subsequent game, the tournament hosts, France, thrashed Iceland with ease. Lineker, himself a former England player, even joined in the trolling of England with the tweet, 'Can't see why we were so critical of England. Look how difficult France are finding it playing against Iceland 🙄.'[122]

The rolling eyes emoji provides an ironic metacomment: it tells us how Lineker intends us to interpret his message – I mean the opposite of what I'm saying here. France are not finding it in the least bit difficult dismantling Iceland in an international soccer game; England should not have found it difficult either; hence, the press criticism of England following their humiliation by Iceland, which has a population of just over 300,000, was entirely justified.

In this way, the emoji tells us that Lineker in fact means the opposite of what his words say; the contradiction is achieved while showing off Lineker's trademark self-deprecating humour. After all, this is the man who made good on his Twitter wager to present the BBC flagship TV soccer highlights show *Match of the Day* in his underwear, if his boyhood football club Leicester City won the league – they did it, and so did he![123]

The notion of an emoji as providing a metacomment, guiding the interpretation of the text, is, in fact, central to the fourth function of Emoji: its complementing function. Nowhere is this function of Emoji more effective than in sidestepping potentially face-threatening situations – a particularly thorny issue in digital communication, when the mitigating effects of our body language (a smile, wink or self-deprecating shrug) are not available to tone down a message. The notion of face, of course, relates to our sense of self-worth and dignity when interacting with others: in essence, our public persona. Our face can be threatened in a range of ways, hence the complex interplay of politeness strategies we adopt on a daily basis to avoid exactly this.[124] No one wants to look a fool, or to be told to do something: this gets our backs up. And this is where politeness markers come in. A *please* or *thank you!* goes a long way to mitigating the face-threatening nature of the demands others place on us. And in face-to-face interactions, a smile or wink can often tone down otherwise face-threatening remarks, evaluations or requests.

In the context of textspeak, Emoji provides an important cue that influences how a face-threatening message should be interpreted, which can often mitigate the potential threat to someone's face in particular contexts. A bald statement of displeasure, or a threat of consequences if a request is not complied with, can be mitigated with an emoji. Moreover, even in the case of threats, Emoji appears to be mean-proof; it's almost impossible to offend using an emoji.[125] Even an angry face emoji is seldom taken too seriously.

Another example of the complementing function of Emoji is the expression of emotional attitude. One common example of this is when the sender includes an emoji at the end of their message to signal how they feel, providing a metacomment on their own message. This works to provide a non-verbal cue as to their attitude towards what they are saying, and, hence, how to interpret their message. The reprimand 'Late again!', followed by a smile or wink, takes on quite a different meaning from the same phrase followed by an angry face. In this way, emojis provide an important cue enabling addressees to better interpret the communicative signals intended in textspeak.

As such, Emoji also nuances the verbal message, steering the addressee towards a particular interpretation achieved in a humorous way. Consider an example of exactly this, making use of the rolling eyes emoji, adapted from a piece by journalist Ashley Fetters, writing in *GQ*:

A: Did they really go home from the bar together?!
Wow. Guess you can't stop true love.

B: Did they really go home from the bar together?!
Wow. Guess you can't stop true love 🙄.[126]

The narrative in A tells a fairly literal story. After a boozy evening, the couple went home together; despite both being the worse for wear you can't stop true love. In B, however, the scenario is completely different. The disapproving mouth and rolling eyes of the emoji tell us that the sender has a completely different meaning in mind: after a boozy evening, the couple went home together; usually they wouldn't find each other attractive – clearly it was the booze, rather than true love, doing the talking.

Emoji also has an emphasising function. When we use an emoji to reinforce a word, as Julie Bishop does in her tweet, this emphasises the idea being expressed, by virtue of the multimodal support the emoji provides. For instance, the linguistic expressions *parliament* and *stellar year* receive support from the addition of emojis. In the case of *stellar* two emojis are used that correspond to the word, thereby accentuating the idea. When thanking staff at the Department of Foreign Affairs and Trade, Bishop uses both the thumbs-up and hand-clapping emojis, emphasising the thanks being conveyed.

Finally, Emoji also exhibits the sixth function, discourse management. The most frequent locations for an emoji to appear in an instant message or a tweet are the beginning or the end. The first position in a message often serves as a response to something else. For instance, when I respond to a message from someone with whom I'm on emoji-terms, I might use a yellow face, such as a smile, to acknowledge their message, or a thumbs-up to signal approval. And the position at the end serves not only to provide a metacomment, thereby helping to guide an interpretation of my words, but also to signal to my addressee that my idea is complete, and won't roll over into a follow-up message. And the emoji, in this way, provides what conversation analysts sometimes refer to as a transition relevance place: in ongoing conversation, we slow down and pause, when we reach the end of an idea.[127] This is the spot where our addressee can take the floor and start talking, without appearing to be butting in. This ebb and flow of transitions in ongoing talk is what characterises a conversation, where two or more people seamlessly take turns to speak. In textspeak, we can signal that the end of a particular message is also the end of a particular thought: nowhere is it clearer that we've finished what we wanted to say than by closing an SMS message with an emoji.

In light of all this, how does this relate to the angry jerk phenomenon with which we began? The answer, perhaps, is obvious. As a significant proportion of the meaning of a communicative message in social interaction derives from non-verbal cues, it stands to reason that digital textspeak – the linguistic mode – conveys only a relatively small proportion of the information we have access to, in email, SMS and other digital exchanges. There's a gaping lacuna in what digital talk alone can convey. Much of the information relating to emotional expression – projection of personality, the nuancing that accompanies words in spoken language – is missing. It's hardly surprising, therefore, that we can all, on occasion, fall foul of the angry jerk phenomenon: a rushed email, or a casual SMS can sound detached, snotty, or worse.

A backward step?

Some argue that Emoji is a step backwards to the dark ages of illiteracy, making us poorer communicators. But this view is nothing more than ill-informed and blinkered cultural elitism. One commentator, guilty of precisely this, and taking a dim view of Emoji, has decried the rise of the now omnipresent emojis in our daily, digital lives. Professional art critic and contrarian Jonathan Jones, writing in the *Guardian*, contends that: 'After millennia of painful improvement, from illiteracy to Shakespeare and beyond, humanity is rushing to throw it all away.' Emoji is, he proclaims, a 'huge step back for humanity'. His derision is clear: 'Speak Emoji if you want. I'll stick with the language of Shakespeare.'[128]

The irony, of course, is that the language of Shakespeare was designed to be performed. And without the paralinguistic cues, the language itself, for all Shakespeare's genius, would remain lifeless, the zombie words of some long-dead white European male. The emotional resonance of Shakespeare's words come from these cues which breathe an interpretation into his plays: was Iago – one of the most inexplicably evil characters to have walked the apron stage – just plain jealous, or did he have a man-crush on the charismatic Venetian general Othello? The meaning derives from the way the words are delivered, their emotional resonance, the ambiguity conveyed, through tone of voice and accompanying gestures and actions. And in analogous fashion, Emoji helps flesh out the meanings they bring to light, clarifying, nuancing and adding to the otherwise arid textspeak of our emotionally abbreviated digital tongue.

One of the flaws with this sort of prejudiced view of Emoji is that it fundamentally misunderstands the nature of communication. Emoji is not relevant for the long form of written communication, for literature, complex prose, and issues of literacy. Emoji's relevance lies in the truncated and otherwise abbreviated digital messages in daily life – the tweets that replicate the thinking aloud that takes place in casual conversation, and the instant chat facility enabled by messaging apps of different types, which we use, increasingly in lieu of brief spoken exchange, to arrange and coordinate our social lives. To assert that Emoji will make us poorer communicators is like saying that using facial expressions in conversation makes your ideas more difficult to understand. The idea is nonsensical. It's a false analogy to compare Emoji to the language of Shakespeare; Emoji is not a replacement for language. Indeed, a robust finding from research I have conducted – and from the research reviewed and presented in this book – is that Emoji actually enables users to better express their emotions, and even appears to help them to become more effective digital communicators.

In addition, research from educational and clinical contexts demonstrates that visual representation, especially pictures, offers a powerful means of communicating and an alternative to spoken or written language, especially among the young, who are less adept language users. For instance, pictures have been used to effectively communicate with children after an operation, when the linguistic mode is diminished as a means of effective communication.[129] Some recent projects have even taken advantage of Emoji expressly because it facilitates more effective emotional expression than text. Examples include a Swedish children's charity that has developed a set of bespoke emojis to help victims of domestic abuse.[130] Another example is that of the educational programme, the Emotes project, which uses emoji-like characters in order to teach children to better express their emotions.[131] The utility and significance of Emoji in a range of educational, recreational and counselling contexts is enormous.

Even adults often find visual representations especially effective, particularly in educational settings. For instance, it's common to hear people recoil from detailed information presented in professional training seminars claiming they can't take anything in as they are a visual learner. Visual learning is recognised by researchers and educators as one of the four basic styles of learning, and arguably the most common learning style among the global population (the other three are auditory, written and kinaesthetic/action-based).[132] It stands to reason that, just as in educational and counselling contexts images and pictures can be an extremely powerful form of communication, so too is Emoji, in our daily world of textspeak.

Today we are most definitely living in the digital age – our lives are interconnected in a virtual world, with people we have often never met, made possible by mobile internet technology. The overwhelming majority of the world's computer-literate users now use Emoji as a daily necessity. It adds levity, emotional expression and personality. And it is personality that oils communication. Not only does Emoji enable us to better express ourselves in our digital lives, it also enables us to keep friends and make new ones. Emoji is more than just happy or sad faces. It has real communicative value, and represents an important step in making our textspeak fit for purpose in our digital lives. For better or for worse, we're all speaking Emoji now.

5

Colourful Writing

Predictive typing has long been a staple of smartphones, and even mobile phones back in the day before they were smart. It works by figuring out for us the words we want to type, based on word initial-letter combinations, and by adapting to an individual's typing habits; predictive text software 'learns' what the phone user most often says, in order to predict what might be coming next. But in 2016, Apple made headlines when it introduced predictive emoji to its operating system update. For the first time, and without having to download an app, owners of iPads and iPhones were able to replace words with emojis when composing an email or message. It works by suggesting an emoji alternative to a word, and also highlights words that can be replaced with an emoji, as a user types (see Figure 16 in the picture section).

And that's not all. The emojis themselves were also supersized, the glyphs having increased threefold in size, when used alone. While this means larger love hearts and winks, to better express our emotional selves, the key advantage is that the detail of the pictogram shines through: now you can clearly see the difference between, say, the relieved face and the smiling face. But the emojis shrink back to their original size when used alongside text, to make possible mixed-modality messages – language and Emoji.

With this move, Emoji was elevated in terms of credentials and significance, empowered as a sort of universal, electronic alphabet that we can use to help us create, adorn and pepper our written messages. With this in mind, Joanna Stern, a journalist for the otherwise strait-laced *Wall Street Journal*, raised eyebrows when she attempted to write an article in Emoji (see Figure 15 in the picture section).

We saw in Chapter 1 that deciphering the meaning of emoji 'sentences' is no mean feat. And this follows because, as we have seen, Emoji is not a true language: it lacks the grammar and vocabulary required to avoid the sort of ambiguity that arises when we put two emojis next to each other. To show you what I mean, take the last two emojis of the first sentence in Figure 15: a thumbs-up and a video recorder. This sequence of emojis could mean: 'I would like a video recorder', 'video recorders are good/useful', or indeed something else. But in fact, here, the author means it to convey this: 'good at expressing oneself in video form'.

While a writing system reflects and represents a spoken language, Emoji is a colourful addition to our writing systems, providing a sort of enhanced alphabet for the digital age. In her essay, Joanna Stern explains how, as she grappled with this new colourful writing, she realised that 'even to just supplement text with emoji, you need to adjust your brain to think visually: how to communicate in cartoon'.[133]

And this gets to the heart of the matter. Writing forms do develop and evolve, in response to our changing needs. While language itself is many hundreds of thousands of years old – spoken language, for instance, probably goes back to a species of ancestral human, *Homo heidelbergensis*, around half a million years ago[134] – writing is a far more recent innovation.

The invention of writing was a big deal in a number of ways. First, it provides the basis for the distinction between prehistory and history: the written record forms the basis for what we can know with some certainty about the past. Indeed, the earliest forms of writing, such as Egyptian hieroglyphs invented a little over 5,000 years ago, were used to record the life, times and deeds of rulers, and, of course, to celebrate religious events and deities.

Second, unlike spoken language, written text enables communication beyond the here and now. Spoken (and signed) language is ephemeral, while writing provides a record that lives on, for other eyes. Moreover, the written word provides a means of communicating with others without being constrained by our degree of physical proximity to others. After all, a written letter can be delivered, in only a few days, to the other side of the world. And with email or instant messaging, the same letter can be delivered virtually instantaneously.

So, if the emergence of writing systems provides added value to linguistic communication, when and how did it develop, and how has writing continued to evolve? More pertinently, in light of the digital revolution, how did Emoji develop? And which aspects of writing systems gave rise to it?

The emotional life of punctuation

While Emoji is a recent phenomenon, the visual expression of emotion and tone of voice has a long and august history. The challenge, of course, is to imbue visual representations of spoken language – writing systems – with the same informational and emotional complexity as spoken language. In classical Greece, the advent of democratic governance ushered in an era dominated by powerful oratory. Writing played second fiddle. During the Golden Age of Athens, around the fifth century BCE, text was written not only without punctuation, but even withoutspacingbetweenwords. The spoken word was viewed as superior, especially in public contexts, including debate. And those who could read had to make do with poring over scripts in order to decipher them.

It wasn't until the third century BCE that a Greek librarian at Alexandria, in Egypt, proposed simple punctuation marks – the comma, colon and what was known as the *periodos* – which were meant to represent breath marks. But the Romans were not fans. While they introduced dots to separate words, they still resisted punctuation. One of the most famous Roman orators, Cicero, declared that the ending of a sentence should be determined 'not by the speaker's pausing for breath, or by a stroke interposed by a copyist, but by the constraint of the rhythm'.[135] And it seems that Roman readers most likely punctuated the written text by murmuring the words aloud, using rhythm to help them parse the content.

It was later, following the fall of Rome, in the era of Christianity that punctuation came into its own. And this was as a consequence of the new importance of the written word, as a means of spreading the word of Christ; the abbots and clerics sought ways to ensure that readers didn't interpret holy texts in novel ways: the sacred meaning had to be preserved. By the sixth century, Christian writers had begun using punctuation to assist with reading holy texts. It was from this time that punctuation began to signal more than simple breath marks. Grammatical meaning began to be conveyed, with the advent of the comma and the full stop. From the seventh century, spaces began to be used consistently between words. Then in the Middle Ages, the colon, semicolon and question mark were developed, signalling further aspects of grammatical meaning. And finally, by the fifteenth century, the emotionally charged exclamation mark arrived.[136]

From this perspective, the function of punctuation in writing systems, including white spaces between words, is a reflex of some of the functions of paralanguage. For instance, the colon and semi-colon indicate how units of text are related semantically, and can even change the meaning in the process. In this they provide an analogous function to prosodic features in speech such as decelerations of different types, and pauses of different lengths, showing how units of speech are related.

The debate over the relative usefulness of the so-called Oxford comma, a requirement of style guides emanating from Oxford University Press, is a case in point. The Oxford comma is the comma used in lists. For instance:

You need eggs, plain flour, and icing sugar.

The Oxford comma frequently divides opinion among grammar

nerds: advocates claim that without it, the result is ambiguity. In the following without the Oxford comma, the sentence may be misunderstood as suggesting that the speaker's parents are Lady Gaga and Humpty Dumpty:

I love my parents, Lady Gaga and Humpty Dumpty.[137]

This is resolved with the Oxford comma:

I love my parents, Lady Gaga, and Humpty Dumpty.

Detractors point out that the Oxford comma is superfluous if such sentences are simply rephrased: *I love Lady Gaga, Humpty Dumpty and my parents.* Whatever one's view, and assuming you even care, the point is surely this: the comma is more than merely a reflex of a pause in speech prosody. Just like prosody, it affects the meaning of a sentence. In short, punctuation provides a mechanism for imbuing written text with some aspects of paralanguage from spoken discourse. And in so doing, punctuation takes its cue from the semantic functions of paralanguage, including discourse management, nuancing and complementing the conventional meaning of the words, and even the emotion conveyed by tone of voice.

The rise of the emoticon

But while this is still some way short of the full range of non-verbal communicative cues available in spoken, face-to-face interaction, written communication just hasn't required this degree of complexity – until recently. This was because written communication has traditionally complemented, rather than run parallel to, spoken interaction, in both use and significance. The world's literary traditions and genres – from poetry to novels, and from educational textbooks to self-help manuals – don't replace everyday acts of communication. Literary works – novels, plays, poetry – and informational written works – textbooks, manuals, and the like – are produced primarily for entertainment or for informing readers on the detail of specific topics; they are consumed in different ways, for different purposes and in different contexts. And other written genres, such as diary-writing, have quite different purposes again, and often may not even be intended for an audience beyond the author.

But as we've already seen, with the advent of digital technology that initiated what is widely considered to be the world's Third Industrial Revolution (see the table below) our social interaction with others is increasingly taking place in digital venues, rather than in face-to-face spoken interactions. Meetings are being increasingly replaced by email exchanges, gossip discussions are replaced by Facebook chats, and partners, friends and family communicate with one another via instant messaging applications, even when in the same dwelling. Taking the UK as a representative example of a digitally connected Western economy, today over 80 per cent of the UK's adult population, classed as aged sixteen or over, has access to the internet, either at home or on a smartphone, while 72 per cent of all adults make use of social media. Collectively, UK adults now spend nearly twenty-two hours per week online, and the trend is on the rise.[138]

Type	Period	Drivers	Description
First Industrial Revolution	1760–1840	New steam and water-powered technologies, notably the steam engine	Period of transition from agrarian/rural to industrial/city-based societies
Second Industrial Revolution	1870–1914	New technological advances, notably electricity and the internal combustion engine	Period during which industry became highly mechanised enabling factory mass production
Third Industrial Revolution (aka 'Digital Revolution')	1980–Today	Advent of digital technology, notably the personal computer, internet and information and communication technologies	The transition from analogue and mechanical devices to digital

The three Industrial Revolutions.

But with the rising popularity of textspeak, made possible by the digital revolution, this raises the very question of how, exactly, to get emotion into our emails and text messages. One way of doing so is to take advantage of the very medium that writing systems make use of: the visual medium. An obvious way of expressing emotion visually is to represent the human demonstration of the emotional experience iconically: a smile, a wink or a sad face.

Just such a strategy has its origins in a proposal made in the United States in the early 1980s that ultimately gave birth to the so-called emoticon: a blend of the words *emotion* and *icon*. The inventor of the world's first such emoticon is often held to be Scott E. Fahlman, a Computer Science Professor at Carnegie Mellon University. In early digital bulletin boards used by computer science staff and students at the university, jokes and pranks were widespread. And following one case where a purported mercury spillage, which was intended as a humorous hoax, was taken seriously, Fahlman proposed using a smiley emoticon:[139]

> I propose that the following character sequence for joke markers:
>
> :-)
>
> Read it sideways. Actually, it is probably more economical to mark things that are NOT jokes, given current trends. For this, use
>
> :-(

While this proposal, from 1982, is the world's first recorded smiley in the digital age, there are, in fact, earlier examples. Something approaching Fahlman's smiley had been proposed as a punctuation mark over a decade earlier by the Russian literary figure Vladimir Nabokov. In an interview published in 1969, in *The New York Times*, Nabokov, the Russian émigré, responded in prickly fashion to a question as to where he ranked among writers of his era. His response was: 'I often think there should exist a special typographical sign for a smile – some sort of concave mark, a supine round bracket, which I would now like to trace in reply to your question.'[140]

Earlier attested examples of the smiley are recorded in *Reader's Digest*, two years before, which attributed the following to one Ralph Reppert, a *Baltimore Sunday Sun* columnist: 'Aunt Ev is the only person I know who can write a facial expression. Aunt Ev's expression is a symbol that looks like this: –) It represents her tongue stuck in her cheek. Here's the way she used it in her last letter: "Your Cousin Vernie is a natural blonde again –)".'[141]

An even earlier example can be found in the American magazine the *Harvard Lampoon*. It is widely reported that in a 1936 article, one Alan Gregg proposed the following symbols for facial expressions: smile (-), laughter (--), frown (#) and wink (*).[142]

But attempts to add emotional expression to text go back to the nineteenth century. In 1881, the satirical magazine *Puck*[143] published typographical symbols to express humour in print publications (see the examples below).

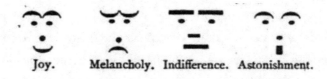

Joy.   Melancholy. Indifference. Astonishment.

Early humour marks as published by *Puck* magazine in 1881.[144]

Further examples abound. The celebrated nineteenth-century journalist, essayist and critic Ambrose Bierce published an essay entitled *For Brevity and Clarity*, in which, with tongue placed firmly in cheek, he argued for writing reform. Bierce, one of the epoch's most celebrated satirists, proposed what he termed a 'snigger point', a line with the ends turned up, with which writers could convey what he referred to as 'cachinnation' – loud or immoderate laughter. As he explained, the snigger point 'is written thus ‿ and presents a smiling mouth. It is to be appended, with the full stop, to every jocular or ironical sentence'.[145] Bierce argued that this would provide 'an improvement in punctuation'.[146]

The most famous, and also most contested, pre-digital emoticon was the emoticon that, perhaps, wasn't. Abraham Lincoln, the sixteenth President of the United States, was a famously witty raconteur. After he gave a speech in 1862, typesetters at the time attempted to capture something of the atmosphere that ensued, in response to the president's particularly droll remarks. They transcribed the audience's applause within parentheses, as follows:

(applause and laughter ;).

It is this mark that has since been pored over by experts in orthography and punctuation, in search of the earliest recorded case of an emoticon. As punctuation expert and historian Keith Houston notes: 'the transcript was typeset by hand, before mechanical typesetting brought with it the risk of gummed-up Linotypes accidentally transposing characters. So it is plausible that ";)" – rather than the more grammatically sensible ");" – was intentional.'[147]

In any case, following Fahlman's intervention in 1982, the use of emoticons quickly took off. Early versions of the internet, such as Usenet – an international electronic discussion forum for personal computer users, established in 1980 – created a medium for electronic communication where discussion required more fine-tuned emotional punctuation than was available in conventional writing systems. And variations on the first emoticons quickly spread. The style adopted, particularly by users of the Latin alphabet, followed Fahlman's lead, with the eyes on the left, then the nose and mouth. In this, the emoticon iconically represents the facial features that stand for the emotional expression it calls to mind. It conveniently uses punctuation marks to provide a visual representation that can easily be interpreted.

A variety of different emoticons emerged in order to signal more nuanced emotional states. Here are some examples:

:-(

This conveys being 'sad'; two turned-down mouth signs represented being 'very sad' or 'weeping':

:-((

Other emoticons include a blush:

'>

A wink:

;-)

A grin:

:-D

And sticking one's tongue out:

:-P

But like any system of communication, emoticons evolve. While Emoticons started out, following Fahlman's lead, with 'noses', as follows:

:-)

There is increasing evidence that some people prefer 'noseless' smiles:

:)

The question is: why?

In order to find out, a researcher examined the use of emoticons by American English users on Twitter, where messages are restricted to 140 characters.[148] Nearly 4 million tweets were examined, which all contained one of the most popular emoticons: the smile, wink, frown and wide smile. The researcher, Dr Tyler Schnoebelen, was especially interested in when emoticons evolve over time, and why, which he investigated as part of his PhD thesis at Stanford University. While both nosed and noseless emoticons are used, it turns out that the noseless variety are far more common. The table below summarises the findings. While the explanation could be that Twitter users simply miss out the nose to save a character, it actually turns out to be both more complicated and more interesting.

Shorthand	Emoticon	Number in the corpus	Percentage of all emoticons in the corpus
Smile	:)	1,496,585	39.6
Wink	;)	397,745	10.5
Frown	: (	312,769	8.3
Big smile	: D	281,907	7.5
Smile/nose	: -)	183,131	4.9
Wink/nose	; -)	70, 618	1.9
Frown/nose	: -(	27,561	0.7

Nosed versus noseless emoticons.[149]

One way in which language changes comes from what's known as 'covert prestige'.[150] While conforming to standard-like ways of speaking is prestigious, sometimes non-standard language can have a hidden, or covert appeal. For instance, swearing among some groups can be a sign of expressing group identity: among young males, swearing rather than, say, using politeness markers is a sign of belonging to the group, and a way of expressing social integrity and in-group membership. This rejection of the social norms of language use in order to belong is a form of in-group or covert prestige.[151]

Following Fahlman's lead, the early uptake and spread of emoticons – especially with the rise of email as a popular means of electronic communication from the early 1990s onwards – featured noses; the nosed variety quickly became established as standard. But the increasing use of noseless emoticons, at least on Twitter – which launched in 2006 – was accompanied by some other interesting features. For instance, tweets from 'non-nosers' tended to be shorter than the tweets from 'nosers'. The non-nosers also used more non-standard spelling conventions: apostrophes were missed in words like *wasn't*; abbreviations like *thru* were used; there were a greater number of typos such as misspelling *tomorrow* as *tomorow*; and non-nosers used exaggerated gestures such as lengthened words to denote emotional affect: *sooo*. These users tended to be younger. In contrast, those who retained the nose tended to be older, produced longer and more standard tweets, with fewer spelling errors.

The pattern seems clear: dropping the nose was an innovation adopted by the young in moving away from an established standard. It seems to be another instance of the covert prestige of non-standard usage: bucking the trend is a sign of being young and rebellious, rather than being perceived as older, boring and more conservative. But of course, since 2012 when this study was conducted, the loss of the nose has continued apace. Many contemporary users of emoticons are today unaware that noses on emoticons were once de rigueur. The irony is that the noseless emoticons, once the preserve of the young and reactionary, today appear to be the new standard.

But of course, emoticons are not emojis. Their significance is that they provided the first step in expressing our emotional selves in the digital age, which set the scene for the later emergence of Emoji. As such, they can be viewed as the precursor of emojis. Emoticons were useful at an earlier point in digital development when the technology that made the display of coloured pictograms possible was still in a fledgling stage. And they were innovative in that they deployed pre-existing punctuation marks in order to provide iconic facial expressions signalling emotion.

The rise of Emoji

With the advent of mobile internet computing users were able, for the first time, to begin to access the internet while on the move, bringing with it new possibilities of instantaneous communication and the consumption of information.

But to approximate the subtlety and range of expression available in face-to-face spoken interaction requires more than the humble emoticon; after all, the emoticon was created for a more rudimentary purpose, in a less technologically sophisticated age of digital communication. Enter Emoji!

The earliest emojis were the brainchild of a Japanese software engineer, Shigetaka Kurita. Kurita – working for NTT DoCoMo one of the largest mobile telephone operators in Japan – was involved in the development of the world's first commercial, mobile-specific internet browser system. Unlike the full internet we take for granted today, early internet-enabled mobile phones, or 'feature phones' as they were known in Japan, could display limited kinds of information, such as weather updates sent directly to the phone via a mobile phone network. The problem was that the Japanese 'feature phones' of the time had a small LCD screen that could only display a maximum of forty-eight characters.

Given these restrictions, Kurita realised that text would be insufficient to display the range of information needed. For instance, in order to convey the idea that the weather is fine, he concluded a symbol of the sun would be more effective and save space: images would provide greater clarity than using text, making the information more accessible in the process. But these early emojis were a far cry from those that we know today. Everything had to be coded digitally, with restrictions on how the images could be displayed. Some examples of Kurita's emoji faces are given below.

A few of Kurita's early emoji faces.[153]

Kurita selected emojis based on the sorts of things users needed to convey and understand. He made use of two sources. The first was the Japanese comic-strip tradition, known as Manga – a tradition that goes back to the nineteenth century.[152] The technique that Manga artists deploy to symbolically represent an idea is known as *manpu*. This uses visual emblems to represent an idea. The emblem might be a visual metaphor, such as when a light bulb over a protagonist's head signals an idea or flash of insight. Alternatively, the emblem might be connected in experience with a particular state, as when a water drop on a face signals nervousness or confusion – nervousness leads to beads of sweat, which are the symptoms of, and stand for, inner turmoil.

The second inspiration for Kurita was infographics – universally used symbols to identify public toilets, parking garages, an emergency exit and places to eat; some of Kurita's infographic-inspired emojis are shown below.

Early infographic-inspired emojis.[154]

Pictograms of this kind had been widely used in Japan since at least the 1964 Tokyo Olympics, to help foreign visitors and athletes. Up until this time, public information signs had been written almost solely in

Japanese. But in fact, these infographics originated in the early part of the twentieth century and they continue to influence data visualisation in our everyday public signage around the world, from airports to highways.

Infographics were invented by Otto Neurath, a Viennese sociologist and philosopher of science, along with his wife Marie, in Austria in the 1920s and 1930s. Neurath was appointed as the founding Director of the Social and Economic Museum of Vienna in 1925. The mission of the new museum was not merely to serve as a repository for physical artefacts, but to actively inform Viennese citizens about their city. Neurath was passionately committed to this notion of a teaching museum. As a result, he pioneered a new visual system to iconically represent complex ideas, bringing dry statistics to life. These, he hoped, would be universally understood, and simple enough to be grasped by schoolchildren. By 1935, the so-called Vienna Method, as the pictorial system of communication had initially been nicknamed, was rebranded as Isotype: International System of Typographic Picture Education.[155] The Neuraths were forced to flee Austria following the rise of Austrian fascism in the 1930s, and settled in the Netherlands, and later the UK. It was in Oxford that they established the Isotype Institute in 1942. Following the Second World War, the ideas generated by the Isotype Institute spread far beyond Western Europe – ranging from Soviet Russia to the United States. It was their extraordinary work that gave rise to the development of modern infographics: the standardised icons developed for public information signage. For instance, in the US, public information signage was formalised in the 1970s by the American Institute for Design.

Infographics standardised by the American Institute for Design
in the 1970s.[156]

In the end, Kurita and his team produced 176 emojis. Kurita's inventory of emojis had two motivations: visual emblems, expressing in particular emotional attitude, and infographics, which expressed more factual information. Figure 17 in the picture section gives Kurita's original emojis.

Three types of writing system

But while Emoji emerged from emoticons, which in turn evolved from systems of punctuation, does this mean that Emoji is somehow fundamentally similar to writing, and might therefore one day replace it? After all, and as we've seen, punctuation was necessitated by systems of writing that lacked the spoken equivalent of paralanguage. Moreover, the rise of punctuation has led, over 2,000 years later, to Emoji, which is increasingly replacing it in textspeak. So, to answer the question whether Emoji can be thought of as a form of writing for the digital age, let's first consider writing, as a system, before returning to Emoji. What makes something a writing system?

Writing systems can be divided into three broad types, referred to by linguists as alphabets, syllabaries and logographies. Alphabetic systems, such as that of classical Greece, the Latin system used in ancient Rome and subsequently adopted throughout former colonies of the Roman Empire, and used for English and many other European languages, has an inventory of letters in which, in general, a letter is meant to correspond to a speech sound. The letters can then be combined to represent linguistic units such as words.

In a syllabary, such as the Japanese Hiragana writing system, each symbol corresponds to a syllable, a group of sounds centring on a vowel sound. For instance, the syllable *ka* is transcribed by a unique symbol. In a syllabic system, the writer is not representing individual sounds with a symbol, but rather a more complex unit of sound. For instance, the English word *hiccup* has two syllables – you can tell, informally, by counting the number of beats as you say the word, hence two symbols would be required in a syllabary system. Some writing systems are a combination of the two. For instance, the Korean writing system, Hangul – literally, the Great Letters of Korea – is an alphabetic syllabary, where alphabetic elements are combined as syllables. Hangul is an especially interesting writing system – invented by King Sejong in the fifteenth century – as there is a near perfect correspondence between symbols used and sounds: the ten simple vowel sounds and fourteen simple consonants are represented by unique symbols. This provides a phonetically accurate writing system that can be mastered very quickly.[157] The joy of Hangul is that once you know how the symbols match up with the sounds, you can learn to read very quickly. This is very different from, say, English, with its wayward spelling, when *trough* and *scoff* have the same final syllables, but are spelled completely differently. During my academic career, I have been fortunate enough to live and work on the Korean peninsula, and soon after arrival I learned to read and write Hangul in just a morning. The only downside was that while I could read the Korean script out loud with ease, I had no idea what my words meant! But the fact that South Korea has an adult literacy rate of around 98 per cent, making it one of the most literate countries in the world, speaks volumes about the value of an intuitive writing system.

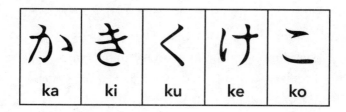

Examples of the Hiragana writing system

What makes Hangul a hybrid between an alphabet and syllabary is that it combines its twenty-four 'alphabetic' symbols into syllabic writing units. Let me show you how this works. Take the name of the writing system, *Hangul*. The Korean symbols for the sounds that make up the word are as follows:

$$\text{ㅎ ㅏ ㄴ ㄱ ㅡ ㄹ}$$
$$\text{H A N G U L}$$

But the symbols are then written as syllable units. There are two syllables in *Hangul*: *han* and *gul*. Hence, the word, in Korean, is transcribed as: *han*: 한, and *gul*: 글, making *Hangul*: 한글.

The final system, logographic, is where a symbol corresponds to an entire word. This is the case in written Chinese and the Kanji script used for Japanese. Many of the Egyptian hieroglyphs were also used as logograms.

One of the major differences between the three systems is the number of symbols that are required. Alphabetic systems generally have fewer, between twenty-five and thirty-five typically, as they provide greater flexibility of combination to build up meaningful units. Syllabaries can have up to a hundred symbols, whereas logographic systems may often require hundreds of symbols.

Is the writing on the wall ... for writing?

So how does Emoji, a system of pictograms – pictorial glyphs representing an idea – compare to a writing system? Well, in fact, and just like Emoji, the world's earliest form of writing started out as a pictographic system.

Writing was invented by the Sumerians, around 3,400 BCE. Sumer was the earliest urban civilisation that we know of, dating from around 6500 BCE. It was located in Mesopotamia – the vast region sandwiched between the Euphrates and Tigris river systems – corresponding roughly to large parts of modern-day Iraq, the southern part of Turkey, as well as taking in parts of Syria and Kuwait. Mesopotamia is often dubbed the cradle of civilisation, having given rise to Sumerian, Akkadian, Assyrian, and Babylonian civilisations.

The Sumer writing system, known as cuneiform, was first developed sometime in the middle of the fourth millennium BCE, but continued to evolve for over 3,000 years, before ceasing to be used during the second century BCE. It began as a pictographic system with around 1,000 signs, before developing its characteristic wedge-shaped signs, of around 400 in total.

The diagram below illustrates the development of the cuneiform writing system, showing how the written form of the Sumerian word *sag*, meaning 'head', evolved between 3000 to 1000 BCE. While in its earliest form, the representation was pictographic, by stage 4, the characteristic wedges were in evidence providing a more abstract means of representing the word. In fact, the word *cuneiform* that we use to name the Sumerian script derives from the Latin for wedge: *cuneus*. With the use of wedge shapes, these could be combined to create a wide array of signs to designate concrete ideas as well as more abstract notions.

Seven stages in the evolution of the representation for 'head' in cuneiform.[158]

In the earliest stages of its evolution, cuneiform was a logographic system: the pictograms at stages 1 (around 3000 BCE) and 2 (around 200 years later), for instance, iconically represent an entire word: the pictogram resembled the entity it represented. But later on, a system of wedge shapes were used to capture the same idea. As such, cuneiform evolved the capacity to use the wedge shapes to capture syllables, and even had the capacity to represent sixteen consonants and four vowel sounds, akin to an alphabet.[159] In so doing, cuneiform evolved from using pictograms to ideograms – abstract visual symbols to represent a given idea.

How does Emoji compare? Quite clearly, as it currently stands, Emoji is pictographic in nature, reminiscent of the earliest stages of the cuneiform writing system. The substitution function of Emoji, which I described in Chapter 4, forms the basis for the predictive Emoji keyboard that is now a feature of the Apple operating system: an emoji can replace a typed word. But, in fact, there are still relatively few emojis, compared to the written words available in a language. This means that Emoji can only be used within a very limited range to replace the written word. At best, Emoji amounts to an early-stage writing system. If Emoji is ever to challenge the written word, then clearly a larger emoji vocabulary will be required.

One way of circumventing the necessity of an enlarged set of pictographs is to transition from a logographic system to a syllabary or an alphabetic system. And this was the path that cuneiform took by transitioning towards ideograms. But alas, for Emoji, this route is not available to it: as things currently stand, Unicode prohibits an emoji from being ideographic in nature; the pictographic nature of an emoji is enshrined in the very approval process for what form emojis are permitted to take (as we shall see in Chapter 7).

Does this mean, then, that Emoji must shed its pictographic nature if it is ever to have a chance of replacing textspeak? Not necessarily. Another early writing system, Egyptian hieroglyphs, were primarily pictographic. Yet they could also function effectively as a syllabic alphabet, similar to Hangul.

Egyptian hieroglyphs, the pictographic writing system, emerged slightly later than cuneiform, and were used to represent ancient Egyptian. The term *hieroglyph* comes from the ancient Greek: *heiros* means 'holy' and *glyphe* means 'writing', hence 'holy writing'.[160] Indeed, hieroglyphs were originally developed to honour the gods and the pharaohs – the divine rulers.[161] By the middle of the third millennium BCE, there were around 800 hieroglyphs; by the time they ceased to be used, having been replaced by the later emergence of alphabetic systems in the Greco-Roman period, they numbered around 5,000.

Hieroglyphs functioned originally as logographs; used in this way they were followed by an upright stroke, to show that an entire word was being symbolised. But the development of hieroglyphs towards the more flexible syllabic and alphabetic types of writing followed a somewhat different trajectory than cuneiform. Rather than the pictograms evolving into more abstract ideograms, ancient Egyptians applied what is known as the rebus principle, by which pictograms could also function phonetically – the correspondence between a symbol and a sound is the basis of an alphabetic system, remember.

Essentially, the rebus principle allows a message to be produced by the sound associated with a picture, rather than by the picture itself. To show you how this works, consider the following example from medieval heraldry, where it was common to use the sound allusion of pictures on flags and shields to stand for a family name. For instance, the heraldry for Walter Lyhart, Bishop of Norwich from 1446 to 1472, in England, was an image of a stag (*hart* is an older word for a male deer) lying down. In this way, a pictographic representation of a 'lying hart', by virtue of the rebus principle, stood for the Lyhart family name.

The rebus principle was the way in which hieroglyphs developed in order to enable the pictograms to represent more abstract ideas. For example, the hieroglyph below represented an Egyptian vulture. If the hieroglyph was followed by an upward stroke, then what was meant was an entire word, hence: *vulture*. But following the rebus principle, the picture could also be used phonetically. The word for Egyptian vulture was pronounced with a glottal stop – similar to the English pronunciation of the two 't's in *bottle* by a speaker of London Cockney. Without the upward stroke, the hieroglyph was read phonetically, as a glottal stop. In this way, hieroglyphs could be combined in order to write, in principle, any Egyptian word – although hieroglyphs were never fully adopted into a true alphabetic writing system.[162]

Egyptian hieroglyph of a vulture.[163]

So what about Emoji? In textspeak, we often apply the rebus principle to use emojis as sounds. An example is when the eye emoji is used, not to signal an eye, but rather, the first person singular pronoun: *I*. For instance, the example here shouldn't prove too challenging to figure out.

I love you **using the rebus principle.**[164]

But while the use of the eye emoji in this way represents the first person pronoun, this still doesn't, alas, amount to a truly alphabetic use of an emoji. After all, the rebus principle allows the eye emoji to substitute for the English word *I*: an entire word. But an alphabetic writing system, in principle, establishes a one-to-one correspondence between a symbol and a sound. Just as the love heart emoji is substituting for the typed word *love*, so too the eye emoji is in effect logographic in nature, using the rebus principle as it applies to a specific language, here English, in order to substitute for an entire word: *I*. What this shows is that the relatively common application to Emoji of the rebus principle remains logographic, rather than truly alphabetic in nature. To be alphabetic we would have to use emojis as sounds, in combination, in order to 'spell' an entire word.

The writing is far from close to being on the wall … for writing. While Emoji has a substitution function in textspeak, it simply doesn't have the characteristics that mean it can replace logographic writing systems – due to impoverished vocabulary – nor can it be used as a syllabic or alphabetic system.

Of course, writing systems such as cuneiform and hieroglyphs developed over millennia. Emoji has only been around for a few years. Nevertheless, in terms of Emoji as writing, the main function, at present, is to add personality, especially in social textspeak, by emojis substituting for words. And there are notable extreme forms of this, as we saw with the article written in emoji for the *Wall Street Journal* with which we began.

I have, on occasion, been pressed into service to write entirely in Emoji. One example relates to work that I conducted on behalf of Barclays Bank plc. This research involved the relationship between language and emojis, based on British attitudes to money. In a survey of how Brits discuss financial relationships, we discovered that 40 per cent of Britons find talking about money more awkward than discussing relationships, or even than bumping into an ex-partner; more than 30 per cent of Brits would rather be out of pocket than ask for money owed to them, while one in five lose in excess of £100 a year for this very reason.

In contrast, we also found that almost half (49 per cent) of young people – respondents aged eighteen to twenty-five – believe that emojis can make a conversation less awkward. To make life a little easier for Barclays' bashful British customers, I was commissioned to translate into Emoji the top finance-related expressions that Brits find most awkward to say (see the table below).

I can't afford it, sorry	
That's too expensive!	
I'm broke	
You owe me money	
You've added that up wrong/ you've miscalculated that	
I don't want to split the bill evenly, I didn't eat or drink	
Can I borrow some money please?	

Finance related expressions translated into Emoji.[165]

But while an exercise such as this is fun, for the most part, Emoji is not akin to a writing system. More often than not, using emojis to replace written text is the exception rather than the norm. That said, Emoji adds more than a splash of colour to our digital alphabet. It provides a visual form of communication that is both resonant and powerful. And this is the issue to which we now turn.

6

A Picture Paints
a Thousand Words

If Facebook were a country, it would be the biggest in the world. With around 1.9 billion active monthly users, it dwarfs China, with a comparatively paltry population of roughly 1.4 billion (see the chart below). Moreover, Facebook has almost double the number of active monthly users compared to all the other most-used social media sites combined: Instagram (600 million), Twitter (317 million) and LinkedIn (106 million). The only platform that comes even vaguely close is the text and photo messaging service WhatsApp, with 1.2 billion monthly active users. And Facebook has achieved this while, perhaps ironically, being banned in China, the world's most populous country.

Facebook had relatively humble beginnings. It grew out of the tradition, among many American universities, of having a 'face book' –

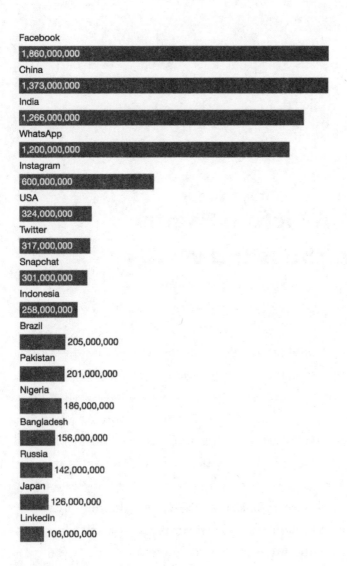

Facebook
1,860,000,000
China
1,373,000,000
India
1,266,000,000
WhatsApp
1,200,000,000
Instagram
600,000,000
USA
324,000,000
Twitter
317,000,000
Snapchat
301,000,000
Indonesia
258,000,000
Brazil
205,000,000
Pakistan
201,000,000
Nigeria
186,000,000
Bangladesh
156,000,000
Russia
142,000,000
Japan
126,000,000
LinkedIn
106,000,000

Numbers of users of social networks and populations of countries. Data as of 2016.[166]

an annually printed directory of students and staff featuring a photograph and biographical information. Back in the early 2000s, Mark Zuckerberg was an undergraduate at Harvard University. The university's move to a web-based 'face book' had been much delayed, due to privacy concerns. And so, Zuckerberg developed his own online version, using images of students he obtained by hacking into university computer servers. While he was forced to take down his original website, and on some accounts narrowly managed to avoid expulsion at a university disciplinary hearing,[167] Zuckerberg subsequently overcame the privacy issues and developed the forerunner of Facebook, known as Thefacebook. It was originally restricted to undergraduates at Harvard, before gradually expanding to encompass all North American universities. Then in 2006, having dropped the 'The', Facebook launched to the general public, for use by anyone thirteen years old or over with an email address.[168]

Facebook's staggering success is underpinned by its use of visuals: images, gifs, auto-playing video clips, and of course photos. More than 300 million images are uploaded onto Facebook every day.[169] And this is what drives usage: images render our communication both more efficient and effective. In today's daily whirl of social media, a text post accompanied by an image is far more likely to receive user engagement – data from the industry-leading eMarketer.com consistently shows that images on social media applications such as Facebook (and Twitter) receive significantly greater comments, shares and retweets than text-only posts.[170]

We are undoubtedly visual creatures. Two popular estimates that often crop up in the blogosphere claim that 90 per cent of external sensory information entering the human brain is visual,[171] and that visuals are processed a whopping 60,000 times more quickly than text.[172] While both these impressive claims may be a little wide of the mark, nevertheless a significant proportion of the human brain is most definitely dedicated to visual processing. When our eyes are open, around two thirds of the brain's neural activity relates to vision,[173] and 40 per cent of the brain's nerve fibres connect to the retina; in fact, more neurons are associated with vision than the four other senses combined.[174] The consequence is that we are very good at processing visual information: it takes around 100 milliseconds to recognise an object,[175] and around 380 milliseconds to perceive a familiar face.[176]

So, might the rapid rise of Emoji have something to do with the fact that visual perception is the dominant sense in our species? And might this explain why visual cues in communication – for instance, kinesics in spoken interaction and Emoji in textspeak – are so effective in helping us better get our message across, and express our emotional selves?

Seeing is believing

Why is visual representation so important in communication? In terms of communicating beyond the here and now, textual representation allows us to overcome the limitations of proximity (as we saw with writing, in the previous chapter). Moreover, for those who suffer from conditions such as cerebral palsy, where speech is impeded due to abnormal development of the brain regions responsible for movement and coordination, visual representation enables communication when spoken language is difficult or impossible.

A case in point is Blissymbolics, a visual language.[177] Blissymbolics is a written form of communication. Yet, unlike other writing systems, it doesn't correspond to a natural spoken language. It was conceived and developed as a language for use solely or primarily in the visual medium. The system was developed by Charles Bliss, an Austrian Jew who was an exile in Shanghai and later Sydney following the Nazi annexation of Austria in the Second World War. He conceived of his visual system as an easy-to-learn 'world-language'. The language was influenced by Bliss's knowledge of Chinese writing characters, and his experiences, in times of upheaval, with different peoples from different backgrounds and cultures, who needed to communicate with one another.

For instance, in Blissymbolics, the English sentence *I want to go to the cinema* would be conveyed as in the diagram below. Reading the sentence from left to right: the Bliss-character for first person singular involves the symbol for person, then the relevant number next to it. The love heart symbol designates a wish or desire, and the small arrow above is an abstract symbol signifying an action – this corresponds to the English verb *to want*. The symbol for *go* is depicted as two legs, and the action symbol above designates that it's an action. The symbol for cinema is a composition of house, picture and an arrow showing a moving picture.

This sentence in Blissymbolics reads *I want to go to the cinema*.[178]

Like other species, we gather information about our everyday world of threat and opportunity through our sensory systems – eyes, ears, mouths, the vestibular system (for our sense of balance), and the haptic and proprioceptive sensors in our skin, tendons and on our joints (for touch and pressure). These sensory systems enable us to harvest different kinds of energy from our external environment.[179] In turn, our brain interprets a variety of different types of energy signals in a way that allows us to make sense of what is happening around us; we can then take action as appropriate. This process of perception is essential as we adapt and react to our environment, in order to find food and shelter, navigate in space, avoid potential threats, and survive and thrive in our environment.

While some species are dominant for sound, such as sonar in bats and echolocation in toothed whales and dolphins, humans are dominant for vision.[180] One famous demonstration of this relates to the relative dominance of hearing and sight. In 1974, psychologist Francis Colavita published now famous results: what has become known as the Colavita 'visual dominance effect'.[181] Colavita presented his subjects with a simultaneous stimulus consisting of both visual and auditory perceptual arrays: a light signal and an auditory tone. While human perceptual apparatus is equally adept at simultaneously perceiving both, subjects were asked to confirm when they had perceived the stimulus by pressing a response key: they could choose from a 'light' key or a 'sound' key. Colavita found that subjects consistently selected the light key in preference to the sound key. This suggests a priming effect: when presented simultaneously with visual and auditory cues, the visual cue wins out, triggering a visual-based response.

This visual dominance effect is part of a more general pattern that psychologists refer to as 'visual capture'. When a visual stimulus is presented simultaneously with auditory and other perceptual stimuli, from different regions of space, the visual stimulus dominates – or captures – the other stimuli. This makes it seem as if the non-visual stimulus originates from the visual source. Other sensory experiences are forced to align with what we're seeing – visual experience trumps auditory stimuli in the brain's hierarchy of sensory processing.

One example of this effect is the ventriloquism illusion. A skilled ventriloquist can create the illusion that a puppet is speaking by 'throwing' their voice. This illusion arises precisely because the audience perceives the auditory stimuli as being 'captured' by the visual experience, which leads to the illusion that the sound derives from the source of the visual stimulus – the puppet's moving mouth.

A famous, and related, illusion is the McGurk effect, so-named after the Scottish psychologist who discovered it in the 1970s. In this illusion, a sound is played to subjects who also watch a person's face on a video screen as they produce an altogether different sound. The visual stimulus of seeing the mouth movements produced for one sound, while actually hearing a different sound, produces an auditory distortion, so that the subjects actually hear a blend of the two sounds, something that sounds more like what they would expect to hear based on the visual experience. This striking effect arises because visual experience can influence what we actually hear. Search for videos of the McGurk effect on YouTube, and see for yourself.[182]

So what accounts for visual dominance in our species? It most likely arises from a long evolutionary trajectory, coming from the sorts of environment our ancestors inhabited. Our ape ancestors evolved and lived for millions of years in the complex and challenging arboreal environment of Africa. Moving amid the treetops required the ability to judge distances between branches in complex treetop canopies. In short, visual experience, and in particular the ability to successfully judge depth, was key to survival, avoiding nasty falls. And even while our hominin ancestors moved down from the trees and began walking upright from around 6 million years ago, the evolutionary engineering that we have inherited, albeit with some significant bells and whistles, is essentially the brain plan of an African ape. And visual dominance is still king.

One line of evidence in support of this idea – that the treetop canopy our forebears once inhabited has shaped our perceptual hierarchy – comes from depth perception, and, more precisely, when we lose the ability to perceive depth. Depth perception arises, in part at least, from something called 'binocular disparity'.[183] By virtue of having two eyes, which are on average 3.5 cm apart in adults, each eye perceives a slightly different aspect of the visual field. Hence, when the light energy harvested by each eye is converted into the electrical nerve signal that the brain works with, the signals are not quite the same. The brain uses the discrepancy between the two to calculate the depth between objects and other entities in our visual field.

One point of interest is that those unfortunate enough to lose sight in one eye suffer difficulties in gauging distance between objects; they also experience difficulty in perceiving in three dimensions, especially closer up, and in terms of rapidly moving objects. For instance, one-eyed people are significantly impaired when it comes to driving and playing tennis. Moreover, loss of vision in one eye leads to visual dominance becoming less acute, with the visual capture effect significantly reduced. Without two effective eyes, human-like visual dominance is undermined.

Emoji as art?

As visual perception has played a central role in the evolution of our forebears, it then seems natural that we read a lot into visual experience: it has pride of place both in conveying information, and in providing aesthetically pleasing experiences. Visual representation has a long and venerable history in our species, and greatly preceded the much later emergence of writing, which depends on it. Indeed, the early writing systems that I discussed in the previous chapter, such as cuneiform and hieroglyphs, originated from artistic traditions, with early written symbols deriving from pictograms. And this, as it turns out, was also the basis for Emoji.

Stone Age paintings date back nearly 40,000 years, with the earliest known cave paintings having been found in Indonesia. The oldest paintings in Europe date to around 30,000 years ago at the Chauvet-Pont-d'Arc Cave in the Ardèche region of southern France, often depict animals and hunting. While Stone Age 'parietal art' – the term for paintings produced on cave walls and ceilings – served as decoration in living spaces, some of the paintings have been found in remote and relatively inaccessible caves with no evidence of habitation, leading experts to believe that they may have served some function in ritualistic ceremonies. While art is often appreciated for its aesthetic value – which varies across time and space, influenced by culture and fashion, as well as understanding and use of technique – art has a number of functions. For present purposes, we can broadly identify three main functions: physical (or instrumental), social and personal.[184]

The physical function concerns the use to which art is put. A Japanese raku hand-held bowl performs a function in a traditional tea ceremony: it serves to mix and hold the tea. But the raku technique, which involves rapid cooling of the fired pottery, enables the precise fixing of colours, resulting in striking artistic effects.

The social function concerns an attempt to influence, comment on, or in some other way intervene in our collective social life. For instance, the graffiti art of Banksy – the anonymous British street artist – is a famous contemporary example.

The personal function is most closely associated with the aesthetic value of art. In this, art can provide self-expression, gratification or entertainment. But these three functions often work in combination, in order to provide a means of communicating an idea, thought, point of view or perspective.

So, in light of this, how art-like is Emoji? Quite clearly, Emoji has an instrumental function: we use it to communicate. In this emojis help us get things done, by nuancing, complementing and even revising the communicative signals we use our words to convey – as we saw in Chapter 4. Emoji also has a social function: it expresses our interpersonal attitude

– how we feel about our addressee, and the content of their message – as well as providing discourse management, enabling us to manage the exchange of text. Finally, Emoji, like art, has a personal function: it signals our personality. Whether we use one (or more) love heart(s) to say *I love you*, whether you send a princess emoji to say sorry for being truculent, or whether you sprinkle your Friday afternoon message with party poppers to say *TGIF*, your decision says a lot about you. And so, just like art, Emoji makes use of the visual mode in order to convey a visually rich (set of) message(s) and evoke an emotional response.

And if I haven't already convinced you of the functional similarities between art and Emoji, for some at least, Emoji is now officially classified as art. In 2016, the New York Museum of Modern Art (MoMA) announced that emojis would be added to its permanent collection. The original 176 emojis, designed by Kurita, shown in Figure 17 in the picture section, have been licensed to the NY MoMA by the Nippon Telegraph and Telephone company (NTT DoCoMo), which originally commissioned them. The emojis now sit alongside works by Pablo Picasso and Jackson Pollock, no less.[185]

In terms of constituting a feat of contemporary visual design that both thoroughly infuses popular culture and peppers our daily electronic exchanges, Emoji has undoubtedly hit the big time. Today, Emoji has achieved a significance, sophistication and ubiquity that Kurita – Emoji's inventor – could never have imagined.

Visual tropes

In Chapter 2, I observed that emojis can be thought of as akin to visual emblems, or tropes. A 'trope' is a literary device designed to have a poetic effect. Here I want to show you, in slightly more technical terms, how this all works. Don't worry too much if some of the details are hard to follow: it's the overall gist of what we're doing when we use and understand an emoji that counts.

The so-called master trope is poetic metaphor: when one idea is used to represent another by virtue of an implied comparison. For instance, upon spying Juliet appearing on her balcony, Shakespeare has Romeo utter the famous lines: 'But soft! What light through yonder window breaks? It is the east, and *Juliet is the sun*.' Here Juliet's beauty is compared with the radiance of the sun. To complete the point, Romeo continues: 'Arise, fair sun, and kill the envious moon, Who is already sick and pale with grief, That thou her maid art far more fair than she.'

But emojis are slightly different from metaphors; after all, strictly speaking they are not comparing anything. Rather, they have more of a referential or pointing function: they draw our attention to a specific idea that the emoji, indirectly, evokes. For instance, a smiling face emoji indicates happiness. But it does so by providing a visual representation of a salient symptom of happiness, a smiling face. In fact, the iconic basis of emojis is often not direct at all. While there is a direct causal link between happiness and smiling, as we saw in Chapter 3, in this the smiley face – the effect – is standing for the cause – the emotional experience that it is a symptom of. This type of trope is known as 'metonymy'. Metonymy is an everyday trope, where one entity stands for another that's causally related to it. For instance, when I say *Buckingham Palace refused to comment*, what I mean is that the British monarch, or their spokesperson, has declined to comment. But Buckingham Palace is causally related to the institution of the monarchy – Buckingham Palace is one of the official residences of the British sovereign. And while this is a linguistic example of metonymy, emojis work in similar fashion – in the visual mode.

That said, visual metonymy involving emojis can be – and often is – significantly more complex still. Let's return to the three wise monkey emojis. As we saw in Chapter 3, they collectively convey a pictorial maxim – in Western culture they are interpreted as an admonition not to turn a blind eye to impropriety. But the emojis, iconically, reflecting the act of covering one's eyes, ears and mouth, evoke different aspects of a complex cause–effect relationship. Were you to place your hands over your eyes, then you cannot see wrongdoing, and thus cannot act to prevent it. And this is so, of course, because placing your hands over your eyes prevents you from seeing anything at all. The consequence is that you are deprived of information from a particular mode of experience: the visual.

In some ways, this is a truism: we can't know what we can't see. When I say *I see what you mean*, what I really mean by this phrase is that I understand. When I say *We need a leader with vision*, I am not advocating that we pack off our leaders for an eyesight test. Rather, I'm bemoaning the perceived lack of a leader – any leader – with a strategy. Knowing something to be the case and seeing that something is the case are inextricably linked, grounded in our experience of the way the world works. And as it turns out, when two things in our everyday encounters are experienced together, they become fused together in our minds. This follows from the way in which our brains learn. Moreover, it's captured by the pithy slogan *What fires together wires together*, associated with the pioneering brain scientist Donald Hebb.[186]

Cognitive scientists George Lakoff and Mark Johnson have argued that pairs of experiences, such as Knowing and Seeing, help provide building blocks for more abstract ideas. Take Time for example. Think about it: there isn't anything in the world that you can point to and identify as time. While we sense its passing, and get glimpses of how it affects us, when we see our ageing faces reflected back at us over the months and years, it is not something we can touch and hold, in the way we can a physical object. Yet we talk about time as if it's an object in motion. We say things like: *The time for a decision has come*, or *Christmas is fast approaching*. And because our experience of time's 'passage' is often experienced when we are in motion from A to B, or perceiving other objects in motion, Time and Motion come to be paired in our minds.

Lakoff and Johnson have famously dubbed pairs of experiences, such as Knowing and Seeing on the one hand, and Time and Motion Through Space on the other, as 'conceptual metaphors'.[187] A conceptual metaphor is different from the metaphoric tropes that we saw with Shakespeare. Rather, what makes something a 'conceptual' metaphor is that it is grounded in our everyday experience of interacting with the world. And these everyday experiences lead to specific patterns in the way our minds are organised. Because we *know* something to be the case whenever we *see* something to be the case, the domains of knowledge we have, relating to KNOWING and SEEING become inextricably linked in our minds. And it is because of this that we can, henceforth, use language relating to seeing, in order to refer to – and be understood to be referring to – knowing and understanding. But importantly, the reverse doesn't follow. These conceptual metaphors have a direction to them. For instance, I can't use language relating to KNOWING in order to refer to SEEING. For instance, I can't say *I know Mount Everest*, and be understood to mean *I see Mount Everest*.

This reveals that while there are links between domains of experience in our minds, the relationships have a direction associated with them. According to Lakoff and Johnson, in the KNOWING IS SEEING conceptual metaphor, the domain of visual experience, SEEING – stated second – provides the target domain, KNOWING, with structure – stated first. In this way, the more abstract idea, KNOWING, receives substance in our minds by drawing upon more tangible and concrete experiences associated with our embodied selves: SEEING. The reason we can talk about leaders with vision, and be understood to be discussing knowledge and wisdom – rather than, say, eyesight and the lack of prescription glasses – is precisely because our minds are structured in terms of the KNOWING IS SEEING conceptual metaphor.

The reason for this brief digression into conceptual metaphors is because the KNOWING IS SEEING conceptual metaphor is important to understanding the metonymic basis for the three wise monkey emojis. The hands-over-the-eyes monkey means that the wise monkey cannot see. And by virtue of not being able to see – a consequence of the logic of the KNOWING IS SEEING conceptual metaphor – the wise monkey cannot know. And this lack of knowing is causally implicated in turning a blind eye to impropriety: a precondition for ignoring impropriety is not to see it. But crucially, the monkey is deliberately covering its face; so the emoji stands for someone who deliberately avoids seeing, and therefore knowing something, in a bid to avoid having to act. In short, while this is a metonymy, the act of covering one's eyes stands for the entire causal chain. And so emojis seem to involve the type of trope known as metonymy: one thing standing for another. But often, this involves one element in a more complex causal sequence.

Of course, things are, perhaps inevitably, a bit more complicated. There are three wise monkeys, not just one. And there are conceptual metaphors for each: KNOWING IS SEEING, KNOWING IS HEARING and COMMUNICATING IS SPEAKING. Each of the three conceptual metaphors – independently motivated by pairs of everyday experiences that become linked in our minds – work together to produce the global pictorial maxim: see no evil, hear no evil, speak no evil.

But, in the case of the eye-covering wise monkey, covering the eyes stands, metonymically, for an entire causal chain, which goes something like this: I am deliberately covering my eyes in order to avoid seeing something that I don't like. If I saw it, I would feel that I had to act, or be morally required to act. But I don't want to have to act (as the action may cause me harm, or be distasteful). Hence, I am choosing to avoid action, by deciding not to see the thing I wouldn't like, and that would require some action from me.

While my explanation of how and why the three wise monkey emojis work may give you a headache, using the emojis – once you get the hang of them – is child's play. Also, once you get to grips with the idea of metonomy, you'll find it at work in loads of emojis. The humble smiley face – the so-called smiling face with open mouth emoji – is metonymic in nature. As I observed previously, a smile is not the same thing as happiness. Rather, a smile is a symptom of happiness. In this way, one outward, physical manifestation of happiness is used, in Emoji, to stand for happiness. Metonymy is, in fact, what makes emojis work!

Seeing emotion

Let's start with the science. Emotions arise from the processing of experiences in mid-brain structures – they give rise to physiological reactions that have evolutionary value. They are homeostatic mechanisms in the body, involving aspects of metabolism, the immune system and impulses, in order to regulate our biological well-being. Their value manifests itself as an instinctive response to a particular situation that poses a threat, such as fear, or provides an opportunity, giving rise to emotional responses that we identify as joy or love. A particular emotion gives rise to a physical state, such a butterflies in the stomach, or increased heart rate, and manifests itself as a 'feeling' – our conscious awareness of emotional states.[188]

What that means is that emotions create an immediate bodily response prompting us to react to a pressing situation; but the advantage is they do so without us having to consciously process the potential options. Without the time lag required to weigh the pros and cons of a particular course of action, emotion kicks in. And hey presto, an action is taken, and dire straits avoided, before thought can screw things up. After all, some events require lightning-fast action; and thought can render us ponderous when a split-second response might save our skin. For instance, the flight or fight response derives from a physiological reaction, involving increased heart rate, the release of adrenalin and other physiological reflexes, that enable the body to respond immediately to a perceived threat or harmful situation, and is often most closely associated with fear.

Researchers distinguish between primary, secondary and even tertiary emotions. Primary emotions are those that emerge developmentally – we are born with them – rather than being learned. These came to be packaged into our genetic heritage over evolutionary time. They are, in some sense, instinctive, not being under voluntary control – in contrast to, for instance, secondary or 'social' emotions, which are, in part, acquired.[189] Primary emotions often precede secondary and tertiary emotions in the heat of the moment and – with apologies to Alfred, Lord Tennyson – in experience, red in tooth and claw.

For instance, the primary emotion anger may often lead to the secondary emotions disgust and rage, rather than vice versa. The table below provides a taxonomy of the various sorts of emotions identified.

While emotion – a biological regulatory mechanism – leads to a feeling – how we consciously experience the emotion – there are also

Primary emotion	Secondary emotion	Tertiary emotions
Love	Affection	Adoration, affection, attraction, caring, compassion, fondness, liking, love, sentimentality, tenderness,
	Lust	Arousal, desire, infatuation, lust, passion
	Longing	Longing
	Optimism	Eagerness, hope, optimism
	Enthrallment	Enthrallment, rapture
	Relief	Relief
Surprise	Surprise	Amazement, astonishment, surprise
Joy	Cheerfulness	Amusement, bliss, cheerfulness, delight, elation, ecstasy, enjoyment, euphoria, gaiety, gladness, glee, happiness, jolliness, joviality, joy, jubilation, satisfaction
	Zest	Enthusiasm, excitement, exhilaration, thrill, zeal, zest
	Contentment	Contentment, pleasure
	Pride	Pride, triumph
Anger	Irritation	Aggravation, agitation, annoyance, grouchiness, grumpiness, irritation
	Exasperation	Exasperation, frustration
	Rage	Anger, bitterness, dislike, ferocity, fury, hostility, hate, loathing, outrage, rage, resentment, scorn, spite, vengefulness, wrath
	Disgust	Contempt, disgust, revulsion
	Envy	Envy, jealousy
	Torment	Torment

Sadness	Suffering	Agony, anguish, hurt, suffering
	Sadness	Depression, despair, gloom, grief, glumness, hopelessness, melancholy, misery, sadness, sorrow, unhappiness, woe
	Disappointment	Disappointment, dismay, displeasure
	Shame	Guilt, regret, remorse, shame
	Neglect	Alienation, defeat, dejection, embarrassment, homesickness, humiliation, insecurity, insult, isolation, loneliness, neglect, rejection
	Sympathy	Pity, sympathy
Fear	Horror	Alarm, fear, fright, horror, hysteria, mortification, panic, shock, terror
	Nervousness	Anxiety, apprehension, distress, dread, nervousness, tenseness, uneasiness, worry

A taxonomy of emotions.[190] Note: Different researchers provide different taxonomies of primary or basic emotions. For instance, Plutchik, an influential emotion researcher, excludes love as a primary emotion.[191]

physical correlates associated with the feeling. These include features of posture, as well as facial expressions, controlled by forty-three facial muscles that give rise to the complex array of expressions symptomatic of emotions of varying kinds. The shape of the mouth, cheeks, eyebrows, as well as eye shape and gaze all provide tell tale signs as to how we are feeling, and are often instantly recognisable.[192] In effect, we actually 'see' the emotional states of others in their posture and facial expressions. And it is these recognisable, outward expressions of emotion that are captured in the yellow emoji faces on our digital keyboards.

Troping the body (with Emoji)

Research within the tradition of conceptual metaphor, pioneered by Lakoff and Johnson, has uncovered a system of metaphors grounded in our experience of the world. With these everyday tropes we can reuse the outward embodied manifestations of emotional states, our feelings, to stand for the emotions they are the physical symptoms of. For instance, with regard to verbal expression, Lakoff and Johnson have shown that we talk and think about happiness and sadness in terms of verticality: *She's feeling up today*; *He's on a high*; *She's down in the dumps*; *I'm feeling low*. The physical posture that co-occurs, in our everyday experience, with being happy or sad is used to represent the emotional state that it is a symptom of.[193] Two domains of experience, physical posture and emotional state, become linked in our minds, in long-term memory – a conceptual metaphor. And, as we saw above, this conceptual metaphor can then be harnessed, metonymically, allowing us to use one idea to point to the closely related idea. The expression *She seems up today* uses the term *up*, which acts as a sort of conceptual reference point for a positive emotional state that the physical posture is an outward expression of.

But we also know that the same conceptual schemes that we use to express emotion in language apply in the visual mode too.[194] Consider, for instance, the Bayeux Tapestry, an eleventh-century embroidered cloth depicting the events surrounding the Norman conquest of England in 1066. The Bayeux Tapestry, an instance of early narrative art,[195] presents hundreds of human figures in a range of circumstances, with a wide assortment of poses and emotional expressions. Specific emotions, such as grief, anger and fear, make use of a type of 'visual vocabulary', drawn from the human expression of emotions, in order to signal these emotions.

For example, in one study, visual linguist Javier E. Díaz-Vera found that bulging eyes were used in the Bayeux Tapestry to metonymically represent fear.[196] He found thirty-two occurrences representing fear. Two types of bulging eyes were used. On the left, in the illustration below, we have a black pupil with a round hole, and on the right, a black pupil without a hole.

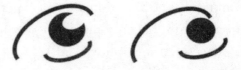

Bulging eyes in the Bayeux Tapestry.[197]

Fig 1. Andy Murray's wedding day tweet.

Fig 2. Quiz on the BBC Newsbeat website. Which of these answers is the correct translation of this emoji sentence?

1. Four climbers find what they think is a dodo chick egg. But it's not. The bird has been extinct for 450 years.
2. One in four people don't know the dodo is extinct, a poll finds.
3. Four children win a science competition to genetically recreate the dodo.

The answer can be found over the page at the bottom of page 3.

Who in the world am I? Ah, that's the great puzzle!

Off with her head!

Fig 3. Quotations from *Alice in Wonderland* translated into Emoji by Joe Hale.

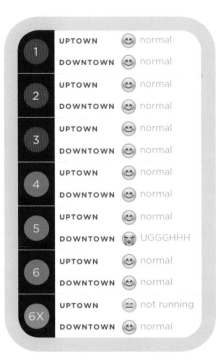

1	UPTOWN	😊	normal
	DOWNTOWN	😊	normal
2	UPTOWN	😊	normal
	DOWNTOWN	😄	normal
3	UPTOWN	😊	normal
	DOWNTOWN	😊	normal
4	UPTOWN	😊	normal
	DOWNTOWN	😊	normal
5	UPTOWN	😊	normal
	DOWNTOWN	😫	UGGGHHH
6	UPTOWN	😊	normal
	DOWNTOWN	😊	normal
6X	UPTOWN	😐	not running
	DOWNTOWN	😊	normal

(***Above***) *Fig 4.* A selection of Finnish national emojis, showing people in saunas, a headbanger and the trusty Nokia 3310 mobile phone.

(***Left***) *Fig 5.* The NYC Live Subway Agony Index, produced by WNYC News, shows travel updates in Emoji.

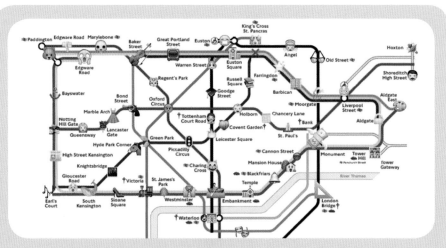

Fig 6. An emojified London Tube Map.

Fig 7. The proposed dumpling emoji.

(**Right**) *Fig 8.* A personalised mail-an-eggplant message.

Fig 9. The gun emoji as depicted on different platforms. From left to right: Microsoft (Windows 10), LG and Apple (iOS 10).

Fig 10. The female singer emoji with dark brown skin is created by combining three different emojis.

Second to the right, and then straight on till morning

Fig 11. Quotation from *Peter Pan* translated into Emoji by Joe Hale, demonstrating a form of Emoji grammar.

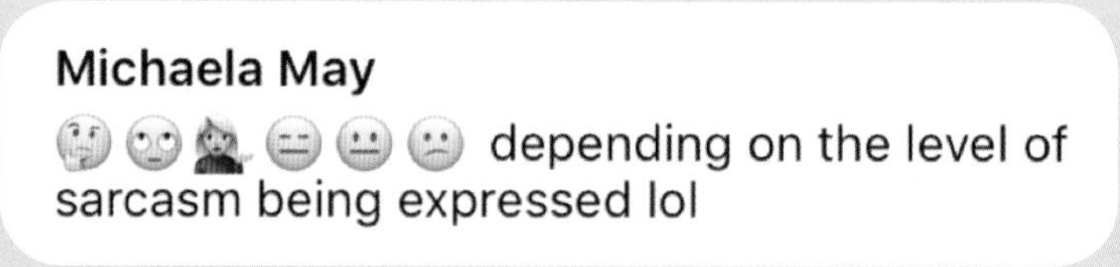

Michaela May

😨 🙄 💁 😑 😐 ☹️ depending on the level of sarcasm being expressed lol

Fig 12. One Twitter user's sarcasm markers.

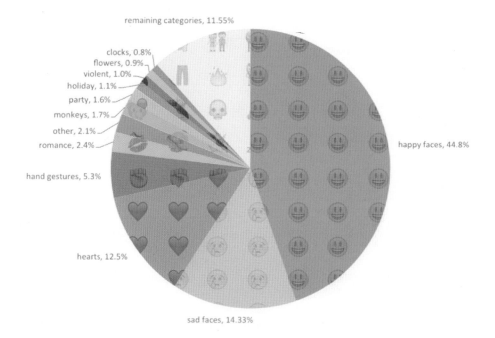

remaining categories, 11.55%

clocks, 0.8%
flowers, 0.9%
violent, 1.0%
holiday, 1.1%
party, 1.6%
monkeys, 1.7%
other, 2.1%
romance, 2.4%

hand gestures, 5.3%

hearts, 12.5%

happy faces, 44.8%

sad faces, 14.33%

(**Above**) *Fig 13*. Pie chart showing the breakdown of emoji usage by category.

Fig 14. Australian MP Julie Bishop's pre-Christmas tweet.

(**Above & above right**) *Fig 15*. The first paragraph from the *Wall Street Journal* article, 'How I learned to love writing with emojis', and accompanying translation.

I was running for the train but I was too late so I've jumped into the car. Not sure if I'll be on time. Hopefully it'll be ok.

I was 🏃, for the 🚆 but I was too late so I've jumped into the 🚗 . 😕 if I'll be on time. Hopefully it'll be 👍 .

(**Above**) *Fig 16*. Predictive emojis at work in Apple's 2016 operating system update.

	Sentence 1	Sentence 2
Line 1	I pride myself at being good at expressing myself in words and even video.	But I am ashamed at how bad I am at writing in emoji.
Line 2	Trying to decipher all these tiny pictures feels like rocket science.	Have you understood any of this article so far, or is it just frustrating?
Line 3	Is this really the future of digital communications?	
Line 4	Nine variations of a cat face?!	Salsa-dancing ladies?
Line 5	But whether we word lovers like it or not, emojis are here to stay.	Their popularity has skyrocketed,
Line 6	and the emoji palette has been growing on smartphones and computers.	
Line 7	So I decided to …	

(**Above**) *Fig 17*. Kurita's original inventory of emojis.

(**Above**) *Fig 18.* Scene from the Bayeux Tapestry, depicting King Harold saving two soldiers from quicksand, and exhibiting the bulging eyes of fear.

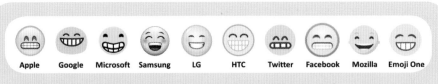

Fig 19. The grinning face emoji across different platforms.

In the scene from the Bayeux Tapestry depicted in Figure 18 in the picture section, King Harold is saving two of his soldiers from drowning in quicksand; he's carrying one soldier on his back and dragging another by the arm. Both Harold and one of the soldiers has bulging eyes, indicating fear. In analogous fashion, compare how different software platforms represent the fearful face emoji; the wide or bulging eyes are also in evidence.

The fearful face emoji as depicted by Apple iOS 9.3 (left) and Google Android 6.0.1 (right).

Similar metonymic schemes, underpinned by conceptual metaphors, are deployed in the visual depiction of emotion, from the animated movies of Walt Disney to comic strips.[198] In this, we deploy visual metaphors – visual symptoms of emotional experience – in order to provide a combination of visual emblems (eye, mouth and eyebrow shape) that metonymically enable facial expressions to stand for, and so point to, specific emotional experiences. Walt Disney understood this better than most. For instance, in the 1939 animated cartoon *The Pointer*, Disney's character Mickey Mouse was already famous. In the short movie, Mickey attempts to teach Pluto, his pet dog, to become a pointer dog. *The Pointer* is often hailed as a landmark in the development of the animated cartoon genre; one innovation was that Mickey Mouse has, among things, pupils added to his eyes.[199] And at a stroke, the changing size and widening of the pupils made more sophisticated emotional expression possible.

In similar fashion, emojis help us to see emotion; moreover, they make emotion real, when we converse in our digital lives. While it may be blindingly obvious that we feel sad, because the emoji looks sad, this doesn't detract from the complex engineering by which we can interpret the sometimes indirect causal chain of events. And so it is in this way that Emoji, as a system of visual communication, can be more effective and more powerful than communication via text alone.

7

All Change for a Changing World

As any professional linguist worth their salt will tell you, language both reflects and helps enact the culture that it is part and parcel of. One obvious way in which this manifests itself is in so-called untranslatable words. These are words that relate to ideas that are culture-specific. The very fact that so many words are untranslatable – there are no equivalent single-word forms for the idea expressed in other languages – only goes to show just how closely aligned language and culture are.

Here are some of my personal favourites. *Tingo* is a word from Pascuan, a Polynesian language spoken on Easter Island. It means: to gradually steal all the items from your neighbour's house, by systematically borrowing but never returning them. *Fernweh*, from German, describes the visceral experience of feeling homesick for a place to which you've never been. The Russian word *toska* is described by Vladimir Nabokov as follows: 'No single word in English renders all the shades of toska. At its deepest and most painful, it is a sensation of great spiritual anguish, often without any specific cause. At less morbid levels it is a dull ache of the soul, a longing with nothing to long for, a sick pining, a vague restlessness, mental throes, yearning. In particular cases it may be the desire for somebody or something specific, nostalgia, love-sickness. At the lowest level it grades into ennui, boredom.' Then there is *cafuné*, from Brazilian Portuguese, which describes the tender act of running one's fingers through your lover's hair. And finally, and perhaps most poignant of all, is *dor*, from Romanian, which describes the intense feeling of loss when you miss a loved one or place that is distant from you.

Just as with language, Emoji is a cultural phenomenon. While Unicode creates an international standard for Emoji, prescribing how any given emoji should be depicted (more or less), the thing is, neither Unicode nor anyone else stipulates what a specific emoji means. As a consequence, the way emojis are used is often due to culture-specific factors.

In Chapter 3 we came across the cultural variation of emojis, when I discussed the different ways in which the two hands pressed together emoji is interpreted, in Japanese versus Western culture. Along the same lines, take the bank emoji. Sometimes this emoji features letters, such as 'bank' or even 'bk' on some software platforms (see examples below). But in Japan, the letters 'bk' often form an abbreviation for the Japanese word *bakkeru*, an idiomatic expression for shirking responsibilities. Thus, in Japanese culture, the bank emoji is often used to signal that someone is slacking off, or otherwise evading their responsibilities.

Another example of cultural variation relates to the two female-themed emojis. While the sexualised bunny suit was developed in the United States by Playboy Enterprises, in the late 1950s, it subsequently became very popular in Japan, where the term *bunnygirl* came to represent a subservient woman with sex appeal, dressed in a bunny suit. Unicode incorporated the emoji in 2010 because an existing Japanese emoji was popular. However, since then, in Western culture it is often used by women to signal friendship, or a girls' night out – a notion that, for most Western women, is far from the emoji's origin. Similarly, the emoji representing a woman holding her hand up as if supporting an invisible tray meant, in Japanese culture, an information desk person. Holding the hand up and out is meant to signal availability to help. But in Western culture, this has come to be reinterpreted as being sassy, and is often used to signal that the preceding remark was intended as being cheeky or sarcastic.

Examples of emojis that mean different things in different parts of the world.[200]

The point is that just as language reflects cultural knowledge and variation, so too do emojis. While emojis provide pictographic representations that are governed by an international, fixed standard, the way we interpret emojis can lead to variation, influenced by our own culture. The irony is that the bunny girl emoji, a cultural reflection of female subservience, adopting a male-oriented sexualised view of women in Japan, has become reinterpreted as an expression of solidarity and even emancipation by women: girls ditching their male partners for a female-only evening.

Emojis, like words, develop new meanings, sometimes far removed from their cultural origins. And like language, Emoji evolves, develops and changes, a consequence of the way it is used, and the uses to which it is put. But, in the way it changes and evolves, how similar to language is Emoji, really?

Language: histories, families and character

Language, like people, is a living, breathing organism that changes and evolves. And just like people, a language has a past, a family – languages also have family trees – and even a particular social status, due to how well heeled a particular language variety is perceived to be.

Let's take English.[201] English is a Germanic language that began to take shape following the arrival of Germanic invaders into Britain from parts of what is, today, the Netherlands, northern Germany and Denmark. The various tribes, the Angles, Saxons and Jutes, that morphed into the English spoke dialects of Old Frisian. In just over a hundred years they had established various kingdoms in what is today England, exploiting the vacuum created by the departure of the Roman legions from Britain around 410 CE. Indeed, the legend of King Arthur is based on a historical figure who united the Romanised Celtic tribes, initially with success, against the threat of these new invaders. But in a cruel twist, the Celts were eventually relegated to the margins of the British Isles: the English words *Wales* and *Welsh* are derived from the Anglo-Saxon term for 'foreign land' and 'foreigner' – the Anglo-Saxon root was *wahla*; in modern German the expression also survives as *welsch*, meaning 'strange'. The irony is that the Welsh, among the original Celtic Britons, were labelled 'foreigners' in their own land by the invading English.

The early settlement patterns of these Germanic invaders have left an indelible mark on English place names. For instance, Sussex, Essex and East Anglia describe present-day regions of England that are abbreviations of once noble Anglo-Saxon kingdoms: South Saxon (Sussex), East Saxon (Sussex) and the land of the Eastern Angles (East Anglia).

But Old English – the English spoken in England until around the time of William the Conqueror in 1066 – is, today, a foreign tongue, barely recognisable to contemporary speakers as English. Consider the following extract, written by Ælfric of Eynsham (955–1010), an abbot and prolific writer in Old English. The following is from his colloquy, a conversation manual from the tenth century intended to help speakers of Old English learn Latin:

We cildra biddaþ þe, eala lareow, þæt þu tæce us sprecan [. . .] forþam ungelærede we syndon & gewæmmodlice we sprecaþ. Hwæt wille ge sprecan? Hwæt rece we hwæt we sprecan, buton hit riht spræc sy & behefe, næs idel oþþe fracod. Wille beswungen on leornunge? Leofre ys us beon geswungen for lare þænne hit ne cunnan. Ac we witun þe bilewitne wesan & nellan onbelæden swincgla us, buton þu bi togenydd fram us.

Here's the modern English translation:

We children ask you, oh teacher, to teach us to speak Latin correctly, for we are unlearned and we speak corruptly. What do you wish to talk about? What do we care what we talk about, as long as the speech is correct and useful, not idle or base. Are you willing to be beaten while learning? We would rather be beaten for the sake of learning than remain ignorant. But we know you to be kind, and you do not wish to inflict a beating on us, unless we force you to it.[202]

While English clearly has a history, with an approximate point of departure – the settlement of several Germanic tribes in that part of Britain that would come to be known as England – it is also part of a larger family of languages. English emerged from the Old Frisian dialects spoken along the North Sea coast running, roughly, from Frisia in the northern part of the Netherlands, along the northern German coast and around the corner and up into the mainland region of Denmark known as Jutland. Due to geographical separation and the essential ingredient, time, a new language slowly emerged. And this new tongue, variously referred to as *Ænglisc*, Anglisc or Englisc – the language of the Angles – had by the seventh century emerged as recognisably distinct from the Frisian tongue of the Continent.

But while English has developed following a different trajectory to its continental counterparts, it nevertheless remains a Germanic language. The ancestral Germanic language – from which all later Germanic languages, including English, derive – is referred to as Proto-Germanic by linguists. While there is no hard, historical evidence for its existence – Proto-Germanic preceded writing systems – it is thought to have emerged in Bronze Age Scandinavia, centring on Denmark and Sweden, around 500 BCE. The Roman historian Tacitus provides anecdotal evidence of Proto-Germanic words in his history of the Germanic tribes, *Germania*, written around 90 CE. By that time, the Germanic peoples, lying just outside the borders of the Roman Empire, had spread down through the North German plain.

As peoples move and are separated by distance and time, change happens. It's typically imperceptible to users of a language, in the daily hurly-burly of life; but over the years and decades, gradual changes add up, leading to quite staggering divergence; and it is such changes that lead to the sorts of striking differences that distinguish Old English (Anglo-Saxon), Middle English (Chaucer), Early Modern English (Shakespeare) and Modern English (today).

There are three branches of the Germanic languages: West Germanic, which includes English, German (with over 100 million native speakers) and Dutch (with around 23 million speakers). North Germanic includes the languages of Scandinavia, such as Norwegian, Danish, Swedish and Icelandic, with around 20 million speakers in total. And finally, there is the extinct East Germanic branch, which included the now dead languages Gothic, Vandalic and Burgundian. The illustration below provides a 'family tree' of the West Germanic branch.

Language also comes in a variety of shapes and forms. Indeed, we might be forgiven for thinking that any given language is one single entity. But in fact, an individual language is made up of a range of different varieties (for instance, American versus Australian versus British versus Irish English); and in this, a language is just like a nation, made up of individual people, with different characters and personalities, which may only bear a passing resemblance to national characteristics.

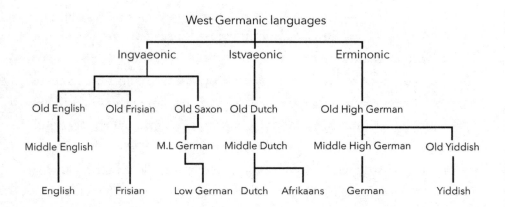

Family Tree of West Germanic languages.[203]

Even the boundaries between individual languages is not always clear-cut. Languages can form a continuum of intelligibility. For instance, speakers of Romanian can more or less understand speakers of standard Italian – both Romanian and Italian are modern-day descendants of Latin. But varieties of the same language can sometimes be mutually unintelligible. While standard British and American varieties of English are mutually intelligible, the English Creole Tok Pisin, spoken in Papua New Guinea, is unintelligible to both.

Even the notion of a standard is a thorny issue. In Shakespeare's time, there was no standard English in the modern sense. The notion of 'standard English' began to take hold later, associated with the language centring on the royal court in London, and influenced by features of midlands English, the most prosperous region of the country at that time. A 'standard' includes features of grammar and vocabulary, as well as accent. The term *Queen's (or King's) English* is often used to refer to standard (British) English, and so-called Received Pronunciation, or RP – a term first used by the British phonetician Daniel Jones in the second edition of his *English Pronouncing Dictionary*, published in 1926 – refers to the accent associated with standard British English. An interesting titbit is that Jones was the real-life prototype for George Bernard Shaw's fictional Professor Henry Higgins, in his play *Pygmalion* – later made into the movie *My Fair Lady*. The film starred Rex Harrison as the professor who could pinpoint any Londoner's place of birth to within two or three streets, just from their accent.

Accent is, perhaps, the most obvious form that a standard can take. But by 1974, only 3 per cent of the population of the United Kingdom spoke RP.[204] Until the 1960s, the BBC eschewed regional varieties – geographical dialects and accents were poor relations compared to RP. In England there is a bewildering array of distinct accents, including Barrovian, Brummie, Bristolian, Cockney, Cornish, Cumbrian, Estuary, Geordie, Lancastrian, Mackem, Mancunian, Northern, Pitmatic,

Potteries, Scouse, Mummerset, with a large number of distinct regional dialects. In the US a wide number of accents and dialects are recognised, including African-American vernacular, Appalachian, Baltimorese, Cajun, Great Lakes, Chicano, Delaware Valley, General American, High Tider, Brooklynese, New York Latino, Old Southern, Ozark, Pennsylvanian Dutch English, Pittsburghese, Yat (New Orleans English) and Yooper, an upper Midwestern dialect, or set of dialects, from the Upper peninsula (hence 'Yooper') of Michigan.

And just to give you a flavour of the further diversity of English, on a global scale there are many distinct regional varieties: Indian English is different from Singlish – the English spoken in Singapore; then there is Strine – the broad Australian accent where the tendency is to run words together. All these varieties of English have different statuses – even within the same geographical region.

For instance, in Singapore, a global city in South East Asia, nearly half of the population comes from outside Singapore; and here, English is the most widely used language. But a caveat is, nevertheless, in order. Singapore uses two distinct varieties: standard Singaporean English, and Singapore Colloquial English, more commonly referred to as Singlish. In 1999, Singapore's then prime minister, Goh Chok Tong, launched a programme to bolster standard English, at the expense of Singlish, among his citizens. This was dubbed the Speak Good English Movement. The point illustrates the way in which a local variety can be viewed as inferior to a standard, even when the local variety, in this case Singlish, is widely adopted.

Emoji: history, family and character

How, then, does Emoji compare? Let's begin by focusing on whether Emoji has any history to speak of. Relatively speaking, Emoji itself doesn't have an extensive history. It was born in a Japanese software laboratory, and saw the light of day in February 1999. Emoji debuted as part of Japanese Telecom giant NTT DoCoMo's mobile internet system: the world's first fully integrated mobile web, known as i-mode. And unlike English, which emerged over long, slow time from earlier Germanic languages, following separation of the Anglo-Saxon tribes from continental Europe, Emoji emerged abruptly. NTT DoCoMo's i-mode achieved 20 million subscribers in Japan following its launch, making Emoji an instant and spectacular success in terms of communicative take-up.

Another way of assessing a communication system's history is to look at its ancestry. As we've seen, a language forms part of a linguistic 'family tree': English can be traced back to Old Frisian, and beyond that to Proto-Germanic. How does Emoji shape up there?

As we saw in Chapter 5, Emoji is related to expressions of emotional attitude in writing systems – emoticons – as well as, more distantly, systems of punctuation. It is also related to the infographics developed in the early part of the twentieth century. And from this perspective, Emoji can be seen as a descendant of both punctuation marks and infographics.

Let's consider the case of punctuation, first, as ancestral to Emoji. I suggested in Chapter 5 that punctuation, in part, enables the expression of paralinguistic cues in the written medium. In particular, punctuation provides an explicit means of expressing emotional attitude, with the exclamation mark originally termed the 'admiration point'. And this earlier term was apt: the exclamation mark is indeed used to express admiration, as well as excitement and other strong emotions.

Moreover, we expect others to signal emotion when they punctuate their writing; and we may even view the lack of punctuation as signalling a lack of empathy and emotional engagement. In an episode from the iconic American sitcom *Seinfeld*, Elaine fights with her boyfriend when he fails to use an exclamation mark in a message he took down for her, following news of the birth of her close friend's baby.[205] She describes his 'troubling' behaviour as evidence he wasn't being sufficiently empathetic. He snarls that he doesn't use exclamation marks willy-nilly, and ends up storming out! While the exclamation mark had been kicking around since the fifteenth century, it only became standard on typewriters in 1970,[206] and then it was only another twelve years before emoticons had developed. But more to the point, the ability to punctuate text with emotional expression, achieved by both, can be viewed as ancestral to the later emergence of Emoji. And from this perspective, Emoji is a descendant of both emoticons and earlier forms of textual punctuation that lie higher up the family tree.

Emoji can also be viewed as being related to pictographic representations of emotion. The infographics that had their origins in 1930s Austria can be seen as precursors to Emoji, as is the *manpu* technique in the Manga tradition; the use of visual emblems of inner, especially emotional, turmoil is a clear ancestor to many of the emojis that were developed by Kurita and launched in 1999. And so we have a number of diverse sources that can be seen as familial precursors to Emoji.

On to the next criterion. Does Emoji, like natural language, undergo change, and how? English has gone through a number of phases, as we've seen, morphing from the Old Frisian dialects of the original invaders, to a distinct English version – Old English – to the Middle, and later, Early Modern Englishes. But in similar terms, Emoji has also evolved. The earliest emojis looked quite different from the glyphs that abound today. Just take a look back at the original emojis from Figure 17. These are a far cry from the first set that were released by Unicode in October 2010.[207] What this reveals is that as technology has evolved, so has our means to represent emojis. Hence, the representation of, ostensibly, the same emoji has also evolved. But it has done so for reasons that are different from the way in which languages evolve.

With regard to language, sounds have come and gone in historically different stages of English: the spelling of *knight*, for instance, reflects how the word was pronounced in Middle English, with the initial *kn* consonant cluster, and the combination of consonants represented by the *gh* and pronounced like the *ch* in the Scottish Gaelic word *loch*, as in *Loch Ness*. But these are sounds and sound combinations that no longer exist in contemporary English – although they, nevertheless, remain in modern German, where the closely related term, *knecht*, which means 'servant', is pronounced exactly as it's spelled. In contrast, emojis have evolved in terms of their visual representation; this is not based on human production, but on our ability to produce technology that provides better opportunities for visual display – more colour, more pixels.

Finally, how does Emoji compare in terms of personality – by analogy, expressed by the different varieties (accents and dialects) of a language, each with its own distinctive character? Emoji, like a language, also has different varieties. While Unicode prescribes a standard, much like Oxford Dictionaries does for standard English, each operating system realises emojis in distinct ways, providing what we might think of as different 'varieties'.

Compare, for instance, the different ways in which the grinning face with smiling eyes emoji is represented across different platforms (see Figure 19 in the picture section). This particular emoji notoriously varies quite significantly. And the fount of all knowledge, with respect to Emoji, the emojipedia.org website, even goes so far as to provide a red-flag warning against it: 'Appearance differs greatly cross-platform. Use with caution.'[208]

The consequence of each platform offering a system-specific variety is the following: the same emoji evokes different responses from users of different platforms – an issue we first touched upon in Chapter 2, in the context of emoji crime. This can be likened to the analogous way in which different varieties of English have a different identity and status, and evoke different reactions – how you speak influences how others see you, as we saw with Singlish.

In Chapter 4, I discussed research that provided a sentiment ranking for the most frequently used emojis. In related, but different, research undertaken at the University of Minnesota in the United States, researchers investigated what they – in this study – dubbed the 'sentiment rating' associated with the visual representation of the same emoji across different platforms.[209] What this means is that depending on features such as mouth shape, eye position, and so on, an emoji can be perceived as conveying a more positive (happier) or more negative (sadder) sentiment.

The purpose of this research was not so much to examine how emojis are ranked against each other, in terms of the sentiment they evoke. Rather, the point was to determine the variation, in terms of sentiment evoked, for the same emoji but across software systems. After all, we have already seen (in Chapter 2) that the gun emoji appears differently on different platforms. Does a difference in appearance of the same emoji evoke a different sentiment?

The research examined twenty-two emojis and found divergence in the sentiment ranking across different platforms. For instance, the grinning face with smiling eyes emoji on the Apple platform was found to have a sentiment ranking of −1, while Android-based platforms had positive sentiment rankings of between 4 and 5. In other words, the sentiment evoked by the same emoji on the Apple platform is neutral or negative, while a more positive emotion is evoked on Android platforms. This is illustrated in the scale below.

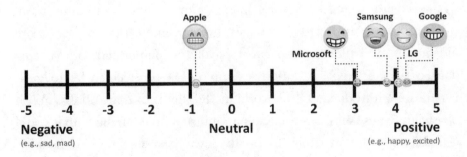

Sentiment ranking for the grinning face with smiling eye emoji across different platforms.[210]

The consequence of this can be potentially confusing. While I might send a grinning face with smiling eyes emoji from my Android smartphone to you on your Apple iPhone, it ends up looking like the variety on the Apple operating system you happen to be using. But as the way the same emoji is rendered is different on your operating system to mine, your emotional response to the same emoji is different to mine. The very same emoji can become lost in translation, across operating systems!

Communication systems: natural, constructed and fictional

Before exploring in more detail how communication systems change, let's first make an important distinction: that between natural versus constructed languages. Languages like English, French, Japanese and Swahili are all natural languages; they have evolved over time, within a community of speakers with a shared culture, in order to facilitate communication. In contrast, constructed languages are invented by one or more individuals, and their genesis can typically be pinpointed to a specific date, period or event. A famous example of a constructed language is Esperanto – introduced to the world in 1887 by L.L. Zamenhof, a Polish physician, whose aim was to create an international language that could be easily learned in order to break down barriers between peoples. The language was named after Zamenhof's pen-name, Doktoro Esperanto, Esperanto meaning 'one who hopes'. Today there are around

100,000 completely fluent speakers of Esperanto, and the number of Esperanto enthusiasts runs into the millions.[211]

Constructed languages are motivated by a number of different factors, including ease of communication, such as Esperanto or Blissymbolics, or to facilitate communication in specific contexts, such as in robotics, where artificial agents learn to communicate with one another. They are also created to provide added realism in fictional worlds, for instance in movies and in literature.

One example is the alien language that features in the box office record-smashing *Avatar* movie, written and directed by James Cameron. *Avatar* is set in the future on the lush planet Pandora, where the indigenous population of the planet is the Na'vi. Their language, as used in the film, was developed by a linguist, Professor Paul Frommer from the University of Southern California. Frommer created a partial language, for the purposes of the film, with a vocabulary of around 1,000 words. In order to make the language sound distinctive and sufficiently alien, he employed sounds that don't exist in English, and thus would appear exotic to an English-speaking audience. While human spoken languages draw from a large inventory of possible human sounds, the number of distinct sounds, dubbed 'phonemes' by linguists, that a language uses varies quite widely. As we saw in Chapter 3, spoken languages range from having as few as eleven distinct sounds – in the Amazonian language Pirahã, where the men use eleven sounds, female Pirahã speakers make use of just ten[212] – to as many as 144. The RP English of the kind that I speak has in the region of fifty distinct sounds, including combinations of vowels known as diphthongs – two-vowel sequences in words like *paid, tow* and *toy* – and triphthongs – three-vowel glide sequences in, for instance, *player* and *loyal*. For Na'vi, Frommer borrowed sounds from languages such as Amharic, spoken in Ethiopia, and Maori.[213] So, while Na'vi might sound alien to speakers of English, in fact it's far from being unearthly.

But some fictional languages are more elaborate, in the sense of being more complete; and some fictional languages even evolve over time. A classic example is the Elvish language Quenya, developed by J.R.R. Tolkien. Tolkien even coined a word, *glossopoeia*, from the ancient Greek, to refer to the activity of inventing languages, complete with their own mythology and culture.

While Quenya features intermittently in several of Tolkien's books, the language and Elvish culture and history are developed in depth in his *Legendarium* – the mythopoetic body of writing that forms Tolkien's background to *The Lord of the Rings*. Tolkien began working on Quenya perhaps as early as 1910 as a schoolboy, but its grammar continued to change and develop over his lifetime, both as he continued to work on it, and due to the histories of the fictional people that spoke the language. In this, Quenya mirrored the ways in which natural languages change over historical time. Yet while Quenya is more developed than Na'vi, nevertheless it still lags far behind a natural language in the semantic range that can be expressed; Quenya's vocabulary remains impoverished, hence it just wouldn't be possible to have a meaningful conversation in the language.

But while, on the face of it, natural and constructed languages appear to be very different, in practice the distinction between them can often become blurred – they tend to form a spectrum, rather than there always being a hard and fast distinction. For instance, a natural language can be controlled so that it becomes more like a constructed language, coerced to conform to particular requirements for specific purposes.

A good example of this is so-called Plain English. The Plain English campaign began in the UK in 1979.[214] Today, the British government adopts the principles of Plain English on all official gov.uk web pages, and in communications and publications by governmental agencies and ministries. Even local authorities and councils throughout the UK are mandated to adopt the principles of Plain English, especially when communicating with members of the public.

Plain English represents a deliberate attempt to make English clearer, by avoiding many idioms, jargon and foreign words, while also keeping grammatical expression and constructions simple and direct. The UK Government's Digital Service sparked controversy when it announced a Latin ban on the UK government's web pages in 2016. Common Latin abbreviations, such as *e.g.*, *i.e.* and *etc.*, will be replaced by English expressions that, it is claimed, are easier to understand.

In contrast, constructed languages can begin the process of becoming natural-language-like, especially as they acquire native speakers. Esperanto is a case in point. Although it was invented, there are multiple cases of children acquiring Esperanto as their mother tongue, and crossing the divide from being an invented to a natural language. For instance, a study published in 1996 found documentary evidence to support 350 individual cases of Esperanto having been acquired as a native language.[215] Just to be clear, a native language is a language acquired during infancy, usually from around twelve months of age, when a cognitively normal child first begins to produce language. If you, like me, are a native speaker of English, this means you can function effortlessly in that language. For instance, you intuitively know that this sentence – *The afraid soldier ran away* – sounds weird, while *The scared soldier ran away* is perfectly fine. Native competence means that you simply know the first sentence to be ungrammatical, without being aware of the complex grammatical knowledge that you carry around with you in your head that makes this so, and without, necessarily, being able to explain what it is that you know. Moreover, when a child is consistently exposed to more than one language, it can develop native competence in two languages. In such cases, the speaker can be said to have two mother tongues, and is classed as being bilingual.

A celebrated case concerns the British academic, lexicographer and musician Montagu Butler. Butler was an early enthusiast of Esperanto, taking up the language in 1905 at the age of twenty-one and acquiring full fluency soon after. He spent much of his life as an active Esperantist advocating for and propagating Esperanto. He was a central figure in the Esperanto Association of Britain and was elected to the Academy of Esperanto in 1948. Perhaps most famously, he raised all five of his children bilingually in Esperanto from infancy.[216] Consequently, they acquired both Esperanto and English as their mother tongues.

A recent study by the American linguist, and my colleague and good friend, Dr Ben Bergen explored the development of Esperanto as a natural language. Bergen examined eight native speakers of Esperanto and found that its grammar had diverged from standard (or invented) Esperanto in a number of ways; a particularly interesting change involved word order.[217] While invented Esperanto has a free word order, using grammatical case as a way of expressing the subject and object of sentences, other languages express the same information using word order. In contemporary English, word order is fairly stable. As we saw in Chapter 3, we use the order of the words to tell us who did what to whom. For instance, *thumb a lift* versus *lift a thumb* mean quite different things precisely because the position of the words *lift* and *thumb* are altered.

But in English, it wasn't always so. As I briefly mentioned in Chapter 3, in Old English, sentence word order was much more flexible. The following sentence from the *Anglo-Saxon Chronicle* written circa 754, *Þa geascode he þone cyning*, literally means: 'Then discovered he the king', where the verb *geascode* comes before the subject *he*, with the object last: *þone cyning*. But just as contemporary English has lost much of its case system, developing a fixed word order (subject-verb-object) pattern, this is precisely what Bergen also found to have taken place with native-speaker Esperanto.

So how does Emoji compare, in terms of the natural/constructed distinction, as a system of communication? By virtue of Emoji having been created by software engineers in a lab in Tokyo, and subsequently reimagined for a global audience by the Unicode consortium in California, it's clearly a constructed system of communication.

But Emoji is highly unusual in one way, even as an invented system of communication: absolutely anyone can propose a new emoji. As we touched on in Chapter 1, there are certain criteria that make an emoji permissable or not, as we shall see later on. But anyone can propose new emojis. In this, the world's global system of communication is truly democratic. Emoji creation is not the preserve of a Tolkien, with extraordinary knowledge of languages and mythologies, or the linguistic expertise of Professor Frommer who created Na'vi, or even the zealous endeavour of the Polish physician L.L. Zamenhof. Emoji is, increasingly, made by the people for the people, reflecting cultural diversity, values and interests. And to this end, Unicode operates a system whereby each proposal for a new emoji or suite of emojis is considered on merit.

The impulse that increasingly drives the selection process is inclusivity. And this can be illustrated with an example. Food emojis can be proposed by anyone. A new taco emoji was inaugurated in 2015, following a PR campaign by Taco Bell, which ran a Change.org online petition that achieved over 30,000 signatures. But it wasn't this PR stunt that influenced the decision by Unicode to approve the new taco emoji. Rather, it was the submission of a proposal, showing in detail how a taco emoji met the needs of would-be users, filling a gap in the popular culture of food. It was this same motivation that led to Unicode accepting a dumpling as a candidate food emoji. Recall the case of the San Francisco businesswoman who campaigned successfully for Unicode to take dumplings seriously.

What this shows is that in one key respect, Emoji is unlike other artificial systems of communication. While there was a single point of creation, which can be traced back to developments in Japan in the late 1990s, Emoji is now a dynamic system that, while controlled, is expanding at a steady rate. An individual Chinese-American businesswoman has as much influence as to what food emojis should appear as an American corporate food-chain giant.

The making of a word

Any communicative system, whether a language such as English or a code such as Emoji, is only as effective, in terms of its expressive power, as the items of vocabulary that populate it. In the case of a language, these are words; in the case of Emoji, it's the individual emojis that make up the code. So the question is, where do these come from?

Sometimes words have a long, illustrious history. The English word *time* has been kicking around for, well, a long time. It existed in the Old Frisian spoken by the Anglo-Saxon invaders of England as *tīd*, referring to an era or period. It has given rise in modern English to *time*, *tide* and *tidings*, among other words.

Sometimes words have a peculiar genesis, based in literary creation. I was once commissioned to do some research on music puns, for an online fast-food company that featured adverts where famous pop jingles were replaced with food puns. For instance, a musical pun based on the famous Guns N' Roses rock anthem became: *Take me down to the jumbo prawn city, where the veg is green and the grills are sticky*; and the Madonna classic, 'Like a Virgin', became: *Like a gherkin … Tried for the very first time*. This work led me to examine the origin of the word *pun*. The earliest attested use is probably around 1644. The term derived from the name of a character in a popular 1641 play, *The Guardian* by Abraham Cowley. In the play, the protagonist, Mr Puny, is noted for his attempts at word play. But the word only began to be used more widely in the eighteenth century, beginning to appear in English dictionaries towards the middle of the 1700s.

Sometimes words seem to emerge from out of thin air. For instance, *jaw* appeared in English, seemingly out of the blue, in the late fourteenth century. One possibility is that it was borrowed from the Old French *jowe*, meaning 'mandible'. Another example, *conundrum*, arrived overnight at the end of the sixteenth century, with an unknown origin. The first recorded use of *conundrum* is from 1596 in a work by Thomas Nashe where it was employed as a term of abuse for a pedant. From there it developed into meaning a pun, and later a riddle, settling on its current meaning, of a puzzling question or problem, from the eighteenth century. The *condundrum* conundrum, so to speak, is that the origin of the word is lost. While the word looks as if it derives from Latin, in fact it doesn't. The Oxford English Dictionary speculates that the word may have originated as a university joke, perhaps as a made-up pun based on a Latin term.

Some common words have even appeared for the first time in the last one hundred years. One of the most famous English words of modern times that lacks any backstory is *jazz*, which was named as the word of the twentieth century by the American Dialect Society. The word appeared as a West Coast American slang term in the early 1900s. The earliest attested usage refers, not to music, but to sport. It was used in reference to a baseball pitcher, in a piece that appeared on 2 April 1912 in the *Los Angeles Times*: "'I got a new curve this year,' softly murmured Henderson yesterday, "and I'm goin' to pitch one or two of them tomorrow. I call it the Jazz ball because it wobbles and you simply can't do anything with it.'" It wasn't, in fact, until 1915 that the notion of ebullient spirit, associated with jazz, began to be applied to music, in Chicago. And from there, the rest is history.

But whether there is a long backstory or none, there are a number of factors that lead to a word being coined. The sociolinguist Professor Jean Aitchison points to three factors: fashion, foreign influence and social need. Words come and go due to fashion. For instance, the term *yuppie* was coined in the early 1980s to describe a new breed of university-educated, upwardly mobile young professionals living near or in cities. The term was an abbreviation of the first letters of the words *young urban professional*, plus *ie*. But today, the word is not as widely used as it once was. It's fallen out of favour, usurped by newer and more fashionable words that overlap with aspects of yuppiedom. These include *hipster* and *millennial*, and *yuccie* – a more recent coinage by blogger David Infante[218] – which refers to a 'young urban creative'. It isn't so much that there are no longer yuppies; rather we choose new ways to describe ourselves, and to pick out different aspects of our professional and social lives to emphasise.

Moreover, fashion can lead to trends becoming entrenched in a language. An example is diminutive formation in Australian English. While all dialects of English use diminutive forms – a shortened word – in Australian English it is far more extensive and systematic, with over 5,000 diminutive forms in regular use, in many cases replacing the original words. And this has led to a new trend in diminutive word formation. The pattern involves a word being shortened, with *a*, *o*, *ie* or *y* being added, based on phonological rules. Some, such as *barbie* (for *barbecue*), *Aussie* (for *Australian*) and *lippy* (for *lipstick*), are well known outside Australia. But others are perhaps less so: *ambo* for *ambulance*, and *arvo* for *afternoon*. It is also common for place names, and even eating and drinking venues, to be abbreviated. For instance, the diminutive for *McDonald's* is *Macca's*, which has been registered as a trademark by McDonald's Australia.

English also bears the mark of foreign influence on its word stock. French and Latin have each contributed around 28 per cent of the English vocabulary, with a further 25 per cent deriving from Germanic, Dutch or Old Norse. Around 5 per cent of the vocabulary comes from ancient Greek, while other languages make up a smaller percentage.[219] The global reach of English has meant that it has absorbed an incredible array of foreign words, showing remarkable flexibility and adaptability, leading to one commentator, John McWhorter, to dub English 'Our Magnificent Bastard Tongue'.

For instance, English has borrowed words relating to trade and navigation from Dutch, such as *skipper*, and from painting, such as *easel*, *landscape* and *still life*. It has borrowed words relating to warfare from Spanish, including *guerrilla* and *flotilla*; from Italian have come words for music like *piano*, words from architecture, such as *balcony*, and politics, such as *fascism*, and even items of apparel such as *umbrella*. Indian words have been borrowed including *bungalow*, *curry*, *jungle* and *shampoo*; there are even Aboriginal Australian words, such as *kangaroo* from Guugu Yimithirr. There are many borrowings from Arabic, Amerindian languages, Yiddish, as well as Russian and other Slavic languages. There are even borrowings from languages as far flung as Japan, with *bonsai*, *karaoke*, *samurai* and, of course, *emoji*.

Finally, words emerge to fill gaps that arise to label new social phenomena. Words that we first met in Chapter 3, such as *metrosexual*, *vape*, *selfie* and *Brexit*, are cases in point. The term *metrosexual* dates from the early 1990s, and was coined to describe a new breed of image-conscious men concerned with appearance and fashion. In 2002, *Salon* published an article on the rise of the metrosexual, identifying David Beckham as being a prime example.[220]

How about Emoji? Although new emojis have to be proposed, usually more than a year in advance of acceptance, the factor that motivates their acceptance is predominantly social need. In this, emoji coinage is language-like: emojis are selected either because they fill a gap in the catalogue of emojis, or because they better enable users to express themselves. But unlike words in language, emojis may not be faddish: emojis that are expected to have a short life expectancy are excluded. So, fashion is not a factor in their selection. Moreover, being a global system of communication, which everyone in principle can contribute to through the Emoji proposal system, then, just as with a mongrel language such as English, the stock of new emojis draws from everywhere, as we shall see.

The making of an emoji

There are a number of factors that are considered by Unicode when determining whether a proposed emoji will see the light of day. These include compatibility, expected usage level, image distinctiveness and completeness. Let's take each in turn.

In some cases, a new emoji is required because widely adopted systems, such as Snapchat or Twitter, feature a bespoke emoji. And these emojis enjoy high usage. In such cases, Unicode determines that the emoji should become available universally, in order to ensure compatibility across operating platforms. For instance, in 2010 Unicode introduced the construction worker emoji purely because it already existed in Japan.

The second factor concerns evidence for a high usage level. There must be evidence of a high expected global usage, or high usage within a specific community of users. For instance, in 2016 a fifteen-year-old Muslim from Berlin proposed a new hijab emoji, which has been accepted as a candidate emoji, making headlines in the process. Indeed, while a range of religious emojis already exist, these mainly relate to venues of worship, such as an emoji for a synagogue (Judaism), a mosque (Islam) and a Shinto shrine (indigenous Japanese religion); there are also emojis for the Kaaba – the cube-shaped shrine that is the focus of Islamic pilgrimages to Mecca – for the Jewish Menorah, or Catholic and Greek Orthodox prayer beads. But there were no emojis relating, specifically, to religious apparel. The hijab was proposed as a compound emoji: it can be combined with human, especially female, heads, and is the headpiece traditionally worn by women in Islamic cultures. Hence, this is likely to be a high-frequency emoji within a specific community of users.

While frequency is important, Unicode is careful as to the nature of the evidence it will accept for frequency. For instance, it disregarded the Change.org petition, promoted by Taco Bell, in its consideration of a new taco emoji. The petition, while achieving an impressive number of signatures, nearly 33,000 in total, formed part of a PR campaign, which was heavily promoted by Taco Bell. And as such was deemed to be an unreliable measure of actual potential usage.

A factor related to frequency concerns whether an emoji has more than one potential use; the more meanings an emoji can potentially have, then, self-evidently, the stronger the case for approving it. For instance, the shark emoji can refer to the animal or, as we've seen, metaphorically, to a huckster, as in the hackneyed expression *My lawyer is a shark*.

Of course, some emojis take on meanings that weren't envisaged. Take the dizzy face: a face looking sick or confused from being spun around too much. On some platforms, such as Microsoft, the eyes are presented as spirals. But on others, such as Apple, they are presented as an 'x'.

The dizzy face emoji as it appears on Apple (left) and Microsoft (right) platforms.

The consequence of depicting this emoji with an 'x' for the eyes is that some users take the emoji to mean, and use it to convey, something that is X-rated, or adult in nature, especially in exchanges concerning sex. This is another example of the way in which emojis, as visual glyphs, can come to develop new meanings. By virtue of being visually complex pictograms, emojis can act as visual metaphors, calling to mind meanings other than those they were originally created to convey.

The third factor relates to image distinctiveness. Unicode takes seriously whether there is an image that is sufficiently distinctive to represent the entity the image is meant to call to mind. For instance, given the existing pot of food emoji 🍲, it's not clear that there is a sufficiently

223

distinctive image for more specific food types that are served or prepared in bowls (such as soup, stews, and the like).

Furthermore, emojis are prohibited from being words. While there are emojis that have word-like elements, including simple words ([NEW] [OK]), these are all, nevertheless, represented pictographically in square boxes, typically with a blue background. Moreover, emojis must be, as far as possible, pictograms rather than ideograms. The difference between the two is that a pictogram bears some iconic relationship with the idea that it symbolises. In contrast, an ideogram is an abstract representation of an idea, established through convention. Hence, an arbitrary symbol such as ⨎, for instance, would not be acceptable as a new emoji.

That said, where an existing ideogram has widespread currency, it can be used as an emoji. The eject emoji is a case in point ⏏.

Another factor concerns completeness: new emojis are approved when they are needed in order to fill a usage gap in current types of emoji. A salient example concerns gender equality. According to one study, women outnumber men in their usage of emojis, with 78 per cent of women being regular users compared to 60 per cent of men.[221] Yet, until recently, there was a gender imbalance in the way women, versus men, were represented in Emoji. Indeed, the veteran American actress Jane Fonda, whose penchant for Emoji is widely known, went so far as to publicly bemoan the gender imbalance in Emoji representation.[222]

Until fairly recently, while there were bride, salsa dancer and bunny-eared twin emojis, men had altogether more serious emojis. There were emojis – all male – for professions ranging from the police to the military.

This was rectified in 2016, with the introduction of both male and female versions of thirty-three existing emojis. It's now possible to send emojis of both male and female runners, men and women getting a haircut, male and female police officers, soldiers, receptionists and more.

This perceived inequity prompted a proposal from Google, submitted to Unicode, to go even further: to extend the range of professions represented in Emoji. Eleven new professions were proposed, with both male and female versions of a scientist, chef, graduate and surgeon emojis, all now incorporated by Unicode. This move for completeness has now levelled the playing field in terms of gender equality and the gender-based diversification of professional roles.

A final example of completeness relates to ethnicity and race. While the default colour for people emojis has been yellow or orange, in 2015 Unicode introduced five additional skin tones, known as emoji 'modifiers'. It's now possible, in addition to selecting any male or female emoji, to do so in one of the five skin-tone types. These are based on the Fitzpatrick scale, an established dermatological scale that classifies human skin colour based not on race but on reflectance to light.

There are also guidelines on what cannot appear in Emoji. Emojis relating to logos or brands are not permitted. And emojis that relate to deities or persons living or dead are prohibited. Finally, the images selected for a new emoji may not be overly specific, but must be generic enough to relate to a category of entities. For instance, the police car emoji is a good example . The emoji must be sufficiently specific to call to mind the category 'police car', but not too specific to rule out the range of police vehicles found across the globe.

But equally, an emoji must not be too general so that it fails to relate to the category in question. For instance, the car emoji is displayed, on most platforms, as a red automobile seen from the side. It is generic enough not to relate to any specific type of car – compact car, saloon (or sedan), sports car, minivan and so on – but not too generic that is also picks out vans, trucks and so on – there are separate emojis, for instance, for delivery truck as well as articulated lorry, fire engine, and so forth.

While Emoji, like a natural language, is a system that enlarges its stock of symbols, in some respects it is strikingly different. For one thing, it is highly democratic in a way that natural languages just aren't. Words in a natural language arise from a complex interplay of factors. While any Tom, Dick or Harriet can coin a new word, the uptake of it is dependent on being successfully spread throughout a particular language community. And this process of propagation is enabled by the many, as well as the few: social leaders, influential literary figures, trendsetters, politicians, journalists, and, in today's online world, YouTube and social media stars.

In contrast, as we saw in Chapter 2, when discussing emoji crime, the influence of the emoji trendsetters can, arguably, be pernicious. This relates to the issue of prescriptivism: while the grammar police might pull their hair out at what they perceive to be the perennial decline of language, language changes and evolves as a function of the usage patterns that eddy and swirl, making up our everyday routines of discourse. In contrast, emojis are restricted, both in what sorts of image can be candidate emojis as well as the semantic range of emojis: the cardinal rule of 'no deities' being a pertinent example. Where does the influence, and the software smarts, become too much, in terms of determining which emojis see the light of day, and hence, which ideas we can or cannot express?

The language mavens

Sometimes, so-called experts get it wrong. The way we communicate and use language is an emotive issue for many educated people; after all, in addition to being the tissue that unites us, language is a sign of identity, and some ill-tempered 'experts', so it seems, are predisposed to see decline everywhere. For instance, at a lecture in public speaking and communication at Victoria University, in Melbourne, one Dean Frenkel recently proclaimed that the Australian accent arose from drunkenness. Writing in the Australian newspaper *The Age*, Mr Frenkel expanded, claiming that 'the Australian alphabet cocktail was spiked by alcohol'. He continued: 'Our forefathers regularly got drunk together and through their frequent interactions unknowingly added an alcoholic slur to our national speech patterns … The average Australian speaks to just two thirds capacity – with one third of our articulator muscles always sedentary as if lying on the couch; and that's just concerning articulation.'[223]

While this view is complete nonsense – the characteristic Aussie accent arose from a mix of various dialects in the early British colony, including convicts and free settlers, drawn from various parts of Britain and Ireland – it points to the following. Educated people make fools of themselves when they pass ill-informed judgement on new developments in language and communication.

And so it is with Emoji. As I observed in Chapter 4, some argue that Emoji is taking us back to the dark ages of illiteracy, making us poorer communicators. And this perspective is not an isolated one. In presenting my research in the broadcast media, I've often been told, sagely, that Emoji really is a substandard form of communication. Some suggest that it self-evidently leads to a drop in spelling and/or reading standards; that it may, in fact, be damaging our ability to communicate; and may even be making us dumber. Unless you're an adolescent, or deranged, so the argument seems to be, stick to proper English.

The reason for remarking on this prejudice, in a chapter addressing how communication systems change, is that it points to a misplaced faith in the timeless, unchanging nature of linguistic standards and the status quo. The prejudice that standards are declining is apparent in many corners of everyday life. The elderly complain that the younger generation no longer have manners; the middle-aged decry the drop in standards of popular music compared to the halcyon days of their idealised youth; and we hear, all around us, the hackneyed complaints that politicians are getting more corrupt than yesteryear, bankers more greedy, and so on. The perception that things are going to pot is an especially emotive issue in the realm of language. This is because language is more than merely a means of communicating. It is the very fabric of our social lives, both reflecting and constituting social life. More than that, it is an act of identity: it is the outward expression of who we are, the culture we live in, and even a means of signalling – whether we want to or not – who we aspire to be.

Each time you or I open our mouths and speak, whether it be to a stranger, neighbour, colleague, lover or friend, we are conveying much more than what the words themselves mean. My choice of words, the way I string them together, my accompanying gestures, body language, my intonation patterns – my accent – even the timbre of my voice, provide subtle, yet important points of reference, which others use to identify, evaluate, label, categorise and judge. These verbal and non-verbal modes, deployed during the act of communication, provide others with cues to who I am, cues that others interpret and use to make assessments and decisions about me, as well as others with whom they interact. And even more than that, a language, like a culture, has a past, which informs the present, and which connects us to a shared and collective history.

In the UK, the erstwhile Secretary of State for Education Michael Gove – a prominent politician and notorious for his later star turn in the successful campaign to take the UK out of the EU – hit the headlines back in 2013. He introduced ten golden rules for the civil servants who managed the UK's Byzantine education system. The 'rules' were meant to serve as a guide for written communication in particular, such as emails. For instance, rule number six states: *Read the great writers to improve your own prose – George Orwell and Evelyn Waugh, Jane Austen and George Eliot, Matthew Parris and Christopher Hitchens.*

While reading the literary greats is doubtless a good thing, do we really want to correspond à la Jane Austen or George Eliot? Presumably not. Not only is the mannered epistolary style of Austen outmoded, you'd actually come across as a bit of a twerp. And the late contrarian Christopher Hitchens, despite his literary brilliance, is not everyone's cup of tea, and he did hold some decidedly odd views.

Ironically, those who advise others how to speak and write often do not follow their own rules. A couple of years later, Gove was at it again. This time as Lord Chancellor, heading up the English Ministry of Justice, Gove issued civil servants with guidelines on grammar usage that reflected his pet peeves. These included edicts such as not to begin a sentence with *however*, and to avoid contractions: use *do not*, rather than *don't*. However, as has been widely reported, there are numerous examples in Gove's own writing (in a former life Gove was a journalist for *The Times* newspaper) where he began sentences with *however*, as I have just done in his honour. And as one commentator has observed: 'it is hard not to begin a sentence, in reply, with the word "however"'.[224]

Indeed, a literary great such as Sir Winston Churchill, who was awarded the Nobel Prize for Literature in 1953, was himself aware of the danger of being overly prescriptive in admonitions on supposedly correct English usage. Churchill, who was notoriously proud of his stylistic flourishes, had a fondness for finishing sentences with a preposition. At one time, grammar guides vehemently forbade this sort of wayward practice. According to *The American Heritage Book of English Usage*, an editor who had rearranged one of Churchill's sentences to banish such an oversight was treated to one of Churchill's famously humorous, and sometimes cutting, put-downs. So the story goes, Churchill's scribbled put-down read: 'This is the sort of English up with which I will not put.'

The first good English usage guide was published in 1770. And the genre has always been wrapped up in a tissue of prescribed usage, the view being that there are standards that, in some profound sense, are immutable and correct. But the reality is anything but. Language changes, a natural consequence of the usage-based pressures that apply to our daily interactions – language, grammar and words are changelings.[225] Change is inevitable, a fact of life, whether we want it or not. And language also changes because we need it to. As we have seen, new words are called for due to new inventions, ideas and ways of living. Yet some commentators hanker after a perceived former golden age of language usage, as if change were a bad thing.

Perhaps the most famous of them all, in terms of arbiters of usage, is L'Académie française. The self-proclaimed *immortels* rule on all matters linguistic, with a firm eye on keeping French pure. But even on a generous interpretation, the results are mixed. English-language horrors such as 'les happy few', and 'je suis destroy', common on the streets of Paris, must presumably have Molière turning in his grave. Nevertheless, what we have seen in this chapter is that all systems of communication, language included, evolve and change. And as new media arise, we require new systems to better empower us to exploit their communicative potential. That is exactly the point of Emoji. Its inexorable rise is not due to more than 2 billion people all being dumb. Its success is precisely because we, as a species, have an instinct to communicate. And in the digital age, the doom and gloomers have got it all wrong. Emoji enables and enhances our communicative smarts. And this is something we should all celebrate.

Epilogue: The Future of Communication

The future is notoriously difficult to predict. For instance, in one scene from the cult classic sci-fi movie *Blade Runner*, the main character Deckard, played by Harrison Ford, is in a bar. He makes a phone call to Rachel, with whom he's falling in love, and invites her to join him for a drink. But while the future Los Angeles involves off-world colonies, cyborgs, or 'replicants' as they are termed, and hover cars, Deckard places the call from a hard-wired phone on the wall. Apparently, foreseeing the invention of mobile phones was a step too far for the 1982 movie.

This issue is even thornier when considering human communication. From the perspective of technological innovation, we are living in a digital age: technology is transforming the ways we communicate with one another, and interact with the world around us. Meanwhile, other technological pipe dreams that were once only the preserve of science fiction are now becoming reality. For instance, John Anderton, the character played by Tom Cruise in the 2002 movie *Minority Report* –

originally a short story by Philip K. Dick, as was *Blade Runner* – wears a data glove, providing a sophisticated gesture-based interface system. But touch-based computing is now de rigueur, with the pinch, pull and swipe features of Apple iPads and iPhones having led the way in the 2000s. In computer gaming, the Wii in 2006, and later, Microsoft Kinect consoles developed similar ways of interacting and controlling virtual characters and actions. Devices such as these are surely but a prelude of what is to come.

MIT computer scientist John Underkoffler predicted, in his 2010 TED talk,[226] that virtual touch-based computing, à la *Minority Report*, is the future of human–computer interfaces; and at the time of writing, he is leading the development of an immersive human–computer interface environment that aims to fully replicate the science fiction of fully intuitive gesture-based systems.[227]

Perhaps an even more exciting area of research, one that will transform how we communicate with computers over the longer term, is so-called brain–computer interfaces. In the 1995 film *Johnny Mnemonic* – a cyber punk action thriller, based on the short story by William Gibson – the protagonist, played by Keanu Reeves, wears a cybernetic brain implant that stores information that can be extracted. Today's research on brain–computer interfaces works on a related idea: the brain makes use of electrical signals – an electrical code – to transmit and process information. For instance, sensory information, such as light and sound, harvested by the eyes and ears is transduced into an electrical nerve impulse that the brain can process. Research on brain–computer interfaces works on the same principle – the idea is that as the brain runs on electrical signals, and assuming these can be accurately read, then the signals should allow us to communicate with external devices via the transmission of electrical impulses directly from the brain. For instance, it should be possible, at least in theory, to harness the brain signals that move your arm and hand to control a robotic arm to, say, pick up a cup of coffee.

Research of this kind is ongoing. It is already becoming possible for amputees to use prosthetic limbs with the aid of computer software; and the aim is to interpret the brain's electric signals – to control action through thought. In research undertaken by the US Government's Defense Advanced Research Projects Agency (DARPA), subjects who have lost limbs are now able to 'feel' sensations, due to electronic communication between 'bionic' prosthetics and the brain. This works by using microprocessors in the bionic limb to 'complete' the brain's neural circuit. Outside such specialised research venues, cochlear implants, allowing the hard-of-hearing to hear, is currently the most widely available use for this technology. The principle enables brain signals to communicate with the implant, thereby overcoming the damaged part of the ear. In the future, it may be possible for implants in the brain to allow us to communicate directly with and control a wide array of devices, using the power of thought alone.

In terms of interpersonal communication, some of the earliest predictions about mobile or virtual communication have come true. The hand-held communicators used by Captain Kirk and Mr Spock in the original 1970s episodes of *Star Trek* are essentially hands-free mobile devices, with Bluetooth earpieces. That said, contemporary mobile phones do, nevertheless, require earth-orbiting satellites; hence, their communication range does not encompass subspace transmission, and as such, is not intergalactic – just yet.

Computers and smartphones now come with fixed cameras as standard. This means that we can see the person we are talking to, in real time – media apps such as FaceTime and Skype are cases in point. The next step, perhaps, is the so-called telepresence robot. These are mobile units that host a camera and speaker that can be controlled remotely by someone whose voice and image can be projected. And the virtual person can not only see, via their remote camera, but also follow around and otherwise interact with the person with whom they are conversing. The scope for teleconferencing, and 'remote' tours of a specific venue, such as visiting a real-estate proposition, a new factory or construction site, are obvious. While today's telepresence robots are not cheap, the cost is likely to come down and the systems will improve as the technology advances.

The rapidly changing face of communication is underpinned by what has been termed the ratchet effect.[228] The idea is that culture provides a complex network of shared knowledge, systems, behaviours and practices. This means that by being born into a given culture, shared knowledge is not something we have to learn anew; rather, and paraphrasing the words of Sir Isaac Newton, we stand on the shoulders of previous generations in order to build up and further advance our knowledge base, including technological developments.[229] Each generation takes the developments of the previous one and extends them; and hey presto, in an increasingly short amount of time, this ratchets up the complexity of the technological advances that see the light of day.

To illustrate, let's take a whistle-stop tour of some of the headline technological developments of the twentieth century. The century began with the infancy of aeroplanes, automobiles and radio; it ended with space rockets, space stations, computers, mobile phones and, in 1997, the advent of wireless (Wi-Fi) internet. The twenty-first century opened with the launch of mobile internet capability, with so-called third-generation or 3G wireless mobile telecommunications. Today, with 4G and beyond, we take the internet-everywhere almost for granted.

But while technology will continue to transform the venues and opportunities for communication, it is unlikely to change the nature of communication itself. And this is because human communication is a consequence of a deep and powerful instinct for cooperation that has been over 2 million years in the making.

In an earlier book, *The Crucible of Language*, I described *Homo sapiens* as the cooperative species.[230] Communication preceded language, in evolutionary terms; and while only humans have language, intentional communication is not unique to our species.

For example, drone bees communicate the direction and distance of food sources to worker bees by producing a complex waggle dance upon their return to the hive. In his pioneering research in the early twentieth century, Karl von Frisch referred to this as *Tanzsprache* or 'dance language'.[231] Various species of monkey have rudimentary means of communicating danger, from ring-tailed lemurs to white-faced capuchin monkeys, and from Campbell's monkeys to Diana monkeys.[232]

For even relatively simple systems of communication to have got off the ground, what must be in evidence, in a wide range of species, is what we might dub an evolutionarily basic cooperative intelligence. In any social species, there are norms and patterns associated with interaction. To function effectively, as part of a group, individual members require the ability to interpret and engage with other members, leading to simple systems of communication, especially in terms of achieving the primary needs of any individual: the need for food, the avoidance of danger and the opportunity to procreate.

But changes in the ecological niche of ancestral humans led to an enhanced mode of cooperative living, with the emergence of a cognitively more sophisticated form of ancestral human, *Homo erectus*, around 1.8 million years ago. And with *Homo erectus* came a more sophisticated mode of thinking. This arose from refinements to the interactional intelligence of our great ape ancestors that led to a new form of interactional smarts: cooperative intelligence. While chimpanzees, with whom we share around 98 per cent of our DNA, understand that other chimps have wishes like their own, their lifestyle remains primarily individualistic rather than fully cooperative. In contrast, our species is inherently cooperative: we achieve far more working together than we ever could alone.

Cooperative intelligence can be characterised by what psychologist Michael Tomasello has dubbed joint or shared intentionality.[233] The hallmark of human smarts is an understanding that others have thoughts, feelings and wishes like ourselves. Moreover, we can engage with and otherwise attempt to influence the thoughts, feelings and wishes of others in order to cooperatively achieve shared goals. Communicative systems, such as language, evolved for exactly this purpose.

All this brings us back to the issue of Emoji. Pulling together the various threads of the book, here is the distilled line of argument

I've presented. Technology is not changing the cooperative impulse that underpins communication. Nor is it changing the principles that undergird systems of communication, those that I discussed in Chapter 2. Rather, technology provides new avenues and opportunities; it provides new channels of communication.

But in certain respects, these channels can be impoverished, initially at least, in terms of current systems of communication. Face-to-face spoken interaction is, as we have seen, multimodal. It is a fully immersed experience, in which participants communicate using the full panoply of modes, and make use of linguistic, paralinguistic, kinesic and visual systems of communication. Patterns of eye gaze and prosody convey different aspects of social meaning that fill out the linguistic meaning.

In contrast, textspeak is impoverished in the multimodality stakes. And this is where Emoji has come into its own; it has begun to allow digital communication to replicate some of the non-verbal communicative cues available to face-to-face interaction. It is not that Emoji represents a step-change in communication; rather, and somewhat more prosaically, Emoji is providing an inevitable step in plugging a gap in a new channel of communication: the digital. Without Emoji, part of what provides a well-rounded communicative message is missing. And given that textspeak is a visual form of representation, it is inevitable that pictographic representations should help provide some of the paralinguistic and kinesic cues. Emoji provides a starting point to provide a multimodal system of communication, fit for purpose, in the digital age. We might speculate on how Emoji will develop – in the short term, animated, avatar-like emojis might be one way in which textspeak can be further enhanced by multimodal cues. Facial expressions and gestures are what make us who we are: let's see it, and not be afraid of seeing it, in Emoji!

Whatever the next stage in the evolution of Emoji, the driver is, ultimately, the cooperative intelligence that makes us the unparalleled communicators we are. Emoji makes us more effective communicators in our twenty-first-century world of communication. Viva Emoji!

Notes

1

1 http://www.mirror.co.uk/3am/celebrity-news/andy-murray-tweets-series-funny-5497718

2 https://www.buzzfeed.com/markdistefano/emoji-plomacy?utm_term=.ccN2Pa25r#.kfKr6QrL0

3 http://www.bbc.co.uk/newsbeat/article/32750820/emoji-news-quiz-of-the-week-15-may

4 http://joehale.bigcartel.com/product/wonderland-emoji-poster

5 http://www.wnyc.org/story/your-subway-agony/

6 The figure of 1,851 emoji characters relates to Unicode 9.0 released in June 2016.

7 Emojipedia is the world's foremost resource site for all things Emoji, founded and curated by Jeremy Burge, a member of the technical subcommittee that adjudicates on proposals for new emojis.

8 https://www.ethnologue.com/language/eng

9 Maddison, A. 2001. *The World Economy: A Millennial Perspective. Development Centre of the Organisation for Economic Co-Operation and Development (OECD).*

10 Taagepera, R. 1997. Expansion and contraction patterns of large polities: Context for Russia. *International Studies Quarterly*, 41/3: 502.

11 http://www.emarketer.com/Article/2-Billion-Consumers-Worldwide-Smartphones-by-2016/1011694

12 https://www.emarketer.com/Report/Worldwide-Internet-Mobile-Users-eMarketers-Updated-Estimates-Forecast-20152020/2001897

13 http://www.emarketer.com/Article/2-Billion-Consumers-Worldwide-Smartphones-by-2016/1011694#sthash.p0P9KU38.dpuf

14 SwiftKey report, April 2015; https://blog.swiftkey.com/americans-love-skulls-brazilians-love-cats-swiftkey-emoji-meanings-report/

15 Source: eMarketer.com

16 Figures accurate as of December 2014. http://blog.instagram.com/post/104847837897/141210-300million

17 Figure reported as of September 2014. http://www.adweek.com/socialtimes/infographic-globalwebindex-instagram/438013

18 Source: https://engineering.instagram.com/emojineering-part-1-machine-learning-for-emoji-trendsmachine-learning-for-emoji-trends-7f5f9cb979ad

19 http://emogi.com/documents/Emoji_Report_2015.pdf

20 The research was commissioned by TalkTalk Mobile, and is reported on at: https://theconversation.com/no-the-rise-of-the-emoji-doesnt-spell-the-end-of-language-42208

21 Emogi report 2015. http://emogi.com/documents/Emoji_Report_2015.pdf

22 Evans, V. 2015. *The Crucible of Language.* Cambridge University Press.

23 https://en.wikipedia.org/wiki/Poe per cent27s_law

24 http://www.telegraph.co.uk/technology/news/6408927/Internet-rules-and-laws-the-top-10-from-Godwin-to-Poe.html

25 https://theconversation.com/no-the-rise-of-the-emoji-doesnt-spell-the-end-of-language-42208

26 http://blog.match.com/2015/02/04/match-presents-the-5th-annual-singles-in-america-study/

27 http://time.com/3694763/match-com-dating-survey-emoji-sex/

Notes

28 https://blog.swiftkey.com/americans-love-skulls-brazilians-love-cats-swiftkey-emoji-meanings-report/

29 Ofcom's 2015 Media Use and Attitudes Report: http://stakeholders.ofcom.org.uk/binaries/research/media-literacy/media-lit-10years/2015_Adults_media_use_and_attitudes_report.pdf

2

30 https://www.theguardian.com/technology/2015/feb/02/can-emojis-really-be-used-to-make-terror-threats

31 http://www.dnainfo.com/new-york/20150203/bushwick/terrorist-charge-dropped-against-teen-accused-of-emoji-threats-police

32 Lakoff, G. and M. Johnson. 1980. *Metaphors We Live By*. University of Chicago Press.

33 Lakoff, G. and M. Johnson. 1980. *Metaphors We Live By* (p. 10). University of Chicago Press.

34 Reddy, M. 1979. The Conduit Metaphor: A Case of Frame Conflict in our Language about Language. In Andrew Ortony (Ed.), *Metaphor and Thought* (pp.284–324). Cambridge University Press.

35 Levinson, S. 1983. *Pragmatics* (p.55). Cambridge University Press.

36 Nagel, T. 1986. *The View From Nowhere*. Oxford University Press.

37 https://eggplantmail.com/

38 www.theguardian.com/lifeandstyle/shortcuts/2016/mar/23/real-life-emoji-sexting-would-you-post-someone-an-aubergine

39 https://www.theguardian.com/technology/2015/apr/29/instagram-ban-eggplant-emoji-sexters-fruity-alternatives

40 Poulton, E. 1890. *The Colours of Animals* (pp.21). Kegan Paul, Trench and Treubner.

41 Grice, H.P. 1975. Logic and Conversation. In P. Cole and J. Morgan (Eds.), *Syntax and Semantics*, vol.3 (pp.41–58). Academic Press; Clark, H. 1996. *Using Language*. Cambridge University Press; Strawson, P.F. 1971. *Logico-linguistic Papers*. Methuen.

42 Harder, P. 2010. *Meaning in Mind and Society*. Mouton de Gruyter.

43 http://wallstreetinsanity.com/30-things-women-say-and-what-they-really-mean/

44 Source: http://edition.cnn.com/2017/01/18/health/emoji-use-personality-traits-study

45 Kress, G. (2010: 79) defines a mode as: 'a socially and culturally shaped resource for making meaning'.

46 Kress, G. 2010. *Multimodality: A Social Semiotic Approach to Contemporary Communication*. Routledge.

47 http://www.bbc.co.uk/news/technology-28677674

48 http://stakeholders.ofcom.org.uk/binaries/research/media-literacy/adults-literacy-2016/Section-4-Digital-media-take-up-and-use.pdf

49 Source: Facebook

50 http://www.dnainfo.com/new-york/20150203/bushwick/terrorist-charge-dropped-against-teen-accused-of-emoji-threats-police

51 Evans, V. 2014. *The Language Myth*. Cambridge University Press; Evans, V. 2015. *The Crucible of Language*. Cambridge University Press.

52 Searle, J. 1969. *Speech Acts*. Cambridge University Press.

53 Clark, H. 1996. *Using Language*. Cambridge University Press; Everett, D. 2012. *Language: The Cultural Tool*. Profile Books; Harder, P. 2010. *Meaning in Mind and Society*. Mouton de Gruyter.

54 http://www.dailystar.co.uk/news/latest-news/481439/Emoji-Bomb-Threat

55 https://www.washingtonpost.com/news/local/wp/2016/02/27/a-12-year-old-girl-is-facing-criminal-charges-for-using-emoji-shes-not-alone/

Notes

56 http://www.mirror.co.uk/news/uk-news/tory-mp-sent-emoji-death-8246136

57 http://www.telegraph.co.uk/news/2016/03/31/frenchman-jailed-for-three-months-for-sending-ex-girlfriend-gun/

58 https://www.theguardian.com/technology/2016/jun/20/apple-rifle-emoji-phones-unicode

59 https://www.buzzfeed.com/charliewarzel/thanks-to-apples-influence-youre-not-getting-a-rifle-emoji?utm_term=.iyEG9rRok#.qe113VNb9

60 http://www.campaignlive.co.uk/article/1372807/future-reading-will-emojis-become-first-universal-language#

61 Goldin-Meadow, S. 2005. *Hearing Gestures*. Harvard University Press.

62 Evans, V. 2015. *The Crucible of Language*. Cambridge University Press.

3

63 Fry, S. 2005. *The Ode Less Travelled*. Arrow.

64 http://www.theguardian.com/technology/2015/nov/17/oxford-dictionary-emoji-word-of-the-year-crying-face

65 http://blog.oxforddictionaries.com/press-releases/announcing-the-oxford-dictionaries-word-of-the-year-2015/

66 The term Brexit was coined by British European lawyer and activist Peter Wilding on 15 May 2012, in his Euractiv blog post: Stumbling towards the Brexit (https://blogactiv.eu/blog/2012/05/15/stumbling-towards-the-brexit/).

67 Evans, V. 2014. *The Language Myth*. Cambridge University Press.

68 Evans, V. 2014. *The Language Myth*. Cambridge University Press.

69 Cited in W. Barnett Pearce. 1989. *Communication and the Human Condition* (p.51). Southern Illinois University Press.

70 Crystal, D. 2003. *The Cambridge Encyclopedia of the English Language*. Cambridge University Press.

71 Spevack, M. 1974. *The Harvard Concordance to Shakespeare*. Belknap Press.

72 Efron, B. and R. Thisted. 1976. Estimating the number of unseen species: How many words did Shakespeare know? *Biometrika*, 63:435–447.

73 Crystal, D. and B. Crystal. 2005. *The Shakespeare Miscellany*. Penguin.

74 http://www.jonathan-sun.com/jonnysun/

75 http://yaleherald.com/news-and-features/covers/loving-the-aliebn/

76 http://www.telegraph.co.uk/technology/2016/05/11/monkey-emoji-could-be-the-greatest-twitter-debate-what-do-they-m/

77 From the Analects of Confucius.

78 Source: Emojis provided free by EmojiOne

79 For instance, Lakoff, G. and M. Johnson. 1980. *Metaphors We Live By*. Chicago University Press; Lakoff, G. and M. Johnson. 1999. *Philosophy in the Flesh*. Basic Books.

4

80 Morin, A. 2015. 8 Biggest Myths About Lying According to the Best Human Lie Detector in the World. *Huffington Post*, 28 October: http://www.huffingtonpost.com/amy-morin/the-8-biggest-myths-about-lying-according-to-the-best-human-lie-detector_b_7568892.html

Notes

81 Ekman, P. 2003. *Emotions Revealed: Recognizing Faces and Feelings to Improve Communication and Emotional Life.* Weidenfeld and Nicolson.

82 https://www.theguardian.com/us-news/2017/jan/15/the-seven-faces-of-donald-trump-a-psychologists-view

83 Byron, K. 2008. Carrying Too Heavy a Load. *Academy of Management Review*, 33/2: 309–327.

84 http://www.dailymail.co.uk/sciencetech/article-436434/Study-reveals-smiley-face-email-confusion.html

85 Willis, J. and A. Todorov. 2006. First impressions: Making up your mind after 100 ms exposure to a face. *Psychological Science*, 17/1: 592–598.

86 Frieder, R.; C. Van Iddekinge and P. Raymark. 2015. How quickly do interviewers reach decisions? An examination of interviewers' decision-making time across applicants. *Journal of Occupational and Organizational Psychology*, 89: 223–248.

87 Goleman, D. 1998. *Working with Emotional Intelligence.* Bloomsbury.

88 https://en.oxforddictionaries.com/definition/empathy

89 Birdwhistell, R. 1970. *Kinesics and Context: Essays on Body Motion Communication.* University of Pennsylvania Press; Birdwhistell, R. 1974. The language of the body: The natural environment of words. In A. Silverstein (Ed.), *Human communication* (pp.203–220). Erlbaum; McDermott, R. 1980. Profile: Ray L. Birdwhistell. *The Kinesics Report*, 2/3: 1–16.

90 Chaplin, W., J. Phillips, J. Brown, N. Clanton and J. Stein. 2000. Handshaking, gender, personality, and first impressions. *Journal of Personal Social Psychology*, 79/1:110–117.

91 Padula, A. (2009). Kinesics. In S. Littlejohn and K. Foss (Eds.), *Encyclopedia of communication theory*. (pp.582–584). Sage Publications.

92 Trager, G. 1958. Paralanguage: A first approximation. *Studies in Linguistics*, 13: 1–12; Trager, G. (1961). The typology of paralanguage. *Anthropological Linguistics*, 3/1: 17–21.

93 Argyle, M., V. Salter, H. Nicholson, M. Williams and P. Burgess. 1970. The communication of inferior and superior attitudes by verbal and non-verbal signals. *British Journal of Social and Clinical Psychology*, 9: 222–231.

94 Argyle, M. 1967. *The Psychology of Interpersonal Behaviour.* Penguin.

95 Argyle, M. 1975. *Bodily Behaviour.* Methuen.

96 Argyle, M. 1988. *Bodily Communication* (2nd ed.). International Universities Press.

97 Mehrabian, A. and M. Wiener. 1967. Decoding of inconsistent communications. *Journal of Personality and Social Psychology*. 6/1: 109–114.

98 Mehrabian, A. and S. Ferris. 1967. Inference of attitudes from nonverbal communication in two channels. *Journal of Consulting Psychology*. 31/3: 248–252.

99 Freidman, H. 1978. The relative strength of verbal versus nonverbal cues. *Personality and Social Psychology Bulletin*, 4: 147–150.

100 Kraut, R. 1978. Verbal and nonverbal cues in the perception of lying. *Journal of Personality and Social Psychology*, 36/4: 380–391.

101 Mehrabian, A. 2007. *Nonverbal Communication.* Haldine.

102 Argyle, M., V. Salter, H. Nicholson, M. Williams and P. Burgess. 1970. The communication of inferior and superior attitudes by verbal and non-verbal signals. *British Journal of Social and Clinical Psychology*, 9: 222–231; De Paulo, B., and R. Rosenthal. 1979. Telling lies. *Journal of Personality and Social Psychology*, 37/10: 1713–1722; De Paulo, 1979; Noller P. 1980. Gaze in married couples. *Journal of Nonverbal Behavior*, 5/2: 115–129.

103 Kreuz, R. J. and S. Glucksberg, S. 1989. How to be sarcastic: The echoic reminder theory of verbal irony. *Journal of Experimental Psychology: General*, 118: 374–386.

104 Source: adfailure.com.

Notes

105 Dews, S. and E. Winner. 1995. Muting the meaning: A social function of irony. *Metaphor and Symbolic Activity*, 10, 3–19.

106 Thompson, D., G. Mackenzie, H. Leuthold and R. Filik. 2016. Emotional responses to irony and emoticons in written language: Evidence from EDA and facial EMG. *Psychophysiology*. 53/7:1054–1062.

107 Filik, R., A. Ţurcan, D. Thompson, N. Harvey, H. Davies and A. Turner. 2016. Sarcasm and emoticons: Comprehension and emotional impact. *The Quarterly Journal of Experimental Psychology*, 69/11. http://dx.doi.or g/10.1080/17470218.2015.1106566.

108 https://twitter.com/crocstar/status/779268059605377024

109 Source: Emojis provided free by EmojiOne.

110 Kralj Novak P., J. Smailović, B. Sluban and I. Mozetič. 2015. Sentiment of Emojis. *PLOS ONE* 10/12: e0144296.

111 Filik, R., A. Ţurcan, D. Thompson, N. Harvey, H. Davies and A. Turner. 2016. Sarcasm and emoticons: Comprehension and emotional impact. *The Quarterly Journal of Experimental Psychology*, 69/11. http://dx.doi.or g/10.1080/17470218.2015.1106566

112 Mehrabian, A. 1971. *Silent Messages*. Wadsworth; Mahrabian, A. 2007. *Non-verbal Communication*. Haldine.

113 Casasanto, D. 2013. Gesture and language processing. In H. Pashler, T. Crane, M. Kinsbourne, F. Ferreira and R. Zemel (Eds.), *Encyclopedia of the Mind* (pp.372–374). Sage Publications.

114 McNeill, D. 2005. *Gesture and Thought*. University of Chicago Press.

115 Ekman, P. and W. Friesen. 1969. The repertoire of nonverbal behavior: Categories, origins, usage, and coding. *Semiotica*, 1: 49–98; Ekman, P. 2004. Emotional and conversational nonverbal signals. In J. Larrazabal and L. Peréz Miranda (Eds.), *Language, Knowledge and Representation* (pp.39–50). Kluwer; see also Matsumoto, D., M. Frank and H.S. Hwang. 2013. *Nonverbal Communication: Science and Applications*. Sage Publications.

116 Cienki, A. 2015. Image schemas and mimetic schemas in cognitive linguistics and gesture studies. In M. Pinar Sanz (Ed.), *Multimodality and Cognitive Linguistics* (pp.417–432). John Benjamins.

117 Casasanto, D. 2013. Gesture. In H. Pashler (Ed.), *Encyclopedia of the Mind* (vol. 1). Sage Publications.

118 Kendon A. 1967. Some functions of gaze-direction in social interaction. *Acta Psychologica*, 26:22–63; Argyle, M. and M. Cook. 1976. *Gaze and Mutual Gaze*. Cambridge University Press.

119 Evans, V. 2010. The perceptual basis of spatial representation. In V. Evans and P. Chilton (Eds.), *Language, Cognition and Space: The State of the Art and New Directions* (pp.21–48). Equinox Publishing.

120 http://thoughtcatalog.com/ellen-scheidt/2014/02/the-etiquette-of-emoji/

121 http://www.gq.com/story/three-years-for-the-eye-roll-emoji

122 https://twitter.com/GaryLineker/status/749684889637756929

123 https://www.theguardian.com/football/video/2016/aug/13/gary-lineker-presents-match-of-the-day-in-his-pants-video

124 Brown, P. and S. Levinson. 1987. *Politeness*. Cambridge University Press.

125 http://nymag.com/daily/intelligencer/2014/11/emojis-rapid-evolution.html

126 http://www.gq.com/story/three-years-for-the-eye-roll-emoji

127 Sacks, H., E. Schegloff and G. Jefferson. 1974. A simplest systematics for the organization of turn-taking for conversation. *Language*, 50: 696–735.

128 http://www.theguardian.com/artanddesign/jonathanjonesblog/2015/may/27/emoji-language-dragging-us-back-to-the-dark-ages-yellow-smiley-face

129 Mesko, P., A. Eliades, C. Christ-Libertin and D. Shelestak. 2011. Use of picture communication aids to assess pain location in pediatric postoperative patients. *Journal of Perianesthesia Nursing*, 26/6: 395–404.

Notes

130 http://www.telegraph.co.uk/women/womens-life/11632916/Domestic-violence-victims-have-abused-emoji-to-help-them-communicate.html

131 http://www.emotes.com/v2/index.php

132 Leite, W., M. Svinicki and Y. Shi. 2009. Attempted validation of the Scores of the VARK: Learning styles inventory with multitrait–multimethod confirmatory factor analysis models. *Educational and Psychological Measurement*, 70: 2323–2339.

5

133 http://graphics.wsj.com/how-i-learned-to-love-writing-with-emojis/

134 Evans, V. 2015. *The Crucible of Language*. Cambridge University Press.

135 Cited in Houston, K. 2014. *Shady Characters* (p.6). Penguin.

136 Houston, K. 2014. *Shady Characters*. Penguin.

137 From Grammarly.com http://www.grammarly.com/blog/2015/what-is-the-oxford-comma-and-why-do-people-care-so-much-about-it/

138 http://stakeholders.ofcom.org.uk/market-data-research/other/research-publications/adults/media-lit-2016/

139 http://www.cs.cmu.edu/~sef/sefSmiley.htm

140 http://www.kulichki.com/moshkow/NABOKOW/Inter11.txt

141 *Reader's Digest*, May 1967.

142 *The Harvard Lampoon*. 1936. Vol. 112 No. 1, 16 September, pp.30–31.

143 *Puck*, 30 March 1881, no. 212, p.65.

144 Source: Wikimedia Commons.

145 Ambrose B. 1912. For Brevity and Clarity. *The Collected Works of Ambrose Bierce, XI: Antepenultimata*, (pp.386–387). The Neale Publishing Company.

146 Ibid.

147 Houston, K. 2014. *Shady Characters*. Penguin.

148 Schnoebelen, T. 2012. Do you smile with your nose? Stylistic variation in Twitter emoticons. *University of Pennsylvania Working Papers in Linguistics*, 18/14. Available at: http://repository.upenn.edu/pwpl/vol18/iss2/14.

149 Schnoebelen, T. 2012. Do you smile with your nose? Stylistic variation in Twitter emoticons. *University of Pennsylvania Working Papers in Linguistics*, 18/14. Available at: http://repository.upenn.edu/pwpl/vol18/iss2/14.

150 Labov, W. 2006. *The Social Stratification of English in New York City (2nd ed.)*. Cambridge University Press.

151 Trudgill, P. 1972. Sex, covert prestige and linguistic change in the urban British English of Norwich. *Language in Society*. 1/2: 175–195.

152 Lent, J. 2001. *Illustrating Asia*. University of Hawaii Press.

153 Evans, V. 2016. The brave new world of emoji. *Cambridge Extra*. 15 July. http://cup.linguistlist.org/academic-books/historical-linguistics/the-brave-new-world-of-emoji-why-and-how-has-emoji-taken-the-world-by-storm/

154 Ibid.

155 Burke, C., E. Kindel and S. Walker. 2014. *Isotype: design and contexts, 1925–1971*. Hyphen Press.

156 Source: American Institute for Design, AIGA.

157 Taylor, I. 1980. The Korean Writing System. In P.A. Kolerers et al. (Eds.), *Processing of Visible Language*. Plenum Press.

Notes

158 Source: Wikimedia Commons.

159 Glassner, J-J. 2003. *The Invention of Cuneiform*. Johns Hopkins University Press.

160 Roger, H. 2004. *Writing Systems*. Blackwell.

161 Krebs, R. and C. Krebs. 2003. *Groundbreaking Scientific Experiments, Inventions, and Discoveries of the Ancient World*. Greenwood Publishing Group.

162 Gardiner, Sir A.H. 1957. *Egyptian Grammar*. Oxford University Press.

163 Source: Wikimedia Commons.

164 Source: Emojis provided free by EmojiOne.

165 Source: Barclays Bank PLC.

6

166 Source: https://www.weforum.org/agenda/2016/04/facebook-is-bigger-than-the-worlds-largest-country/

167 http://www.thecrimson.com/article/2003/11/19/facemash-creator-survives-ad-board-the/

168 Lee, N. 2014. *Facebook Nation (2nd ed.)*. Springer.

169 https://zephoria.com/top-15-valuable-facebook-statistics/

170 See one summary of this date here: http://www.socialmediaexaminer.com/photos-generate-engagement-research/

171 Jensen, E. 2008. *Brain-Based Learning (2nd ed.)*. Corwin.

172 http://www.business2community.com/digital-marketing/visual-marketing-pictures-worth-60000-words-01126256#ACpiXMmrah8uv6GB.97.

173 Fixot, R. 1957. *American Journal of Ophthalmology*, vol. Aug.

174 Medina, J. 2014. *Brain Rules*. Pear Press.

175 Liu, H., Y. Agam, J. Madsen and G. Kreiman. 2009. Timing, timing, timing: Fast decoding of object information from intracranial field potentials in human visual cortex. *Neuron*, 02.025.

176 Ramon, M., S. Caharel and S. Rossion. 2011. The speed of recognition of personally familiar faces. *Perception*, 40/4:437–449.

177 www.blissymbolics.org.

178 Source: Wikimedia Commons.

179 Evans, V. 2010. The perceptual basis of spatial representation. In V. Evans and P. Chilton (Eds.), *Language, Cognition and Space: The State of the Art and New Directions* (pp.21–48). Equinox Publishing.

180 Posner, M., M. Nissen and M. Klein. 1976. Visual dominance: An information processing account of its origins and significance. *Psychological Review*, 83/2: 157–171.

181 Colavita, F.B. (1974). Human sensory dominance. *Perception & Psychophysics*, 16/2: 409–412.

182 McGurk, H. and J. MacDonald. 1976. Hearing lips and seeing voices. *Nature*, 264: 746–748.

183 Evans, V. 2010. The perceptual basis of spatial representation. In V. Evans and P. Chilton (Eds.), *Language, Cognition and Space: The State of the Art and New Directions* (pp.21–48). Equinox Publishing.

184 Gombrich, E.H. 1999. *The Uses of Images: Studies in the Social Function of Art and Visual Communication*. Phaidon Press.

185 http://uk.reuters.com/article/us-usa-new-york-emojis-idUKKCN12Q2SQ

Notes

186 Hebb, D. 1949. *The Organization of Behavior*. Wiley and Sons.

187 Lakoff, G., and M. Johnson. 1999. *Philosophy in the Flesh*. Basic Books; see also Evans, V. 2015. *The Crucible of Language*. Cambridge University Press.

188 Damasio, A. 1999. *The Feeling of What Happens: Body and Emotion in the Making of Consciousness*. Harcourt.

189 Damasio, A. 1995. *Descartes' Error*. Picador.

190 Shaver, P., J. Schwartz, D. Kirson and C. O'Connor. 2001. Emotional Knowledge: Further Exploration of a Prototype Approach. In G. Parrott (Eds.), *Emotions in Social Psychology: Essential Readings* (pp.26–56). Psychology Press.

191 Plutchik, R. 1980. A general psychoevolutionary theory of emotion. In R. Plutchik and H. Kellerman (Eds.), *Emotion: Theory, Research, and Experience: Vol. 1. Theories of Emotion* (pp.3–33). Academic Press.

192 Garrod, J. and P. Schyns. 2014. Dynamic facial expressions of emotion transmit an evolving hierarchy of signals over time. *Current Biology*, 24/2: 187–192.

193 See also Kövecses, Z. 2000. *Metaphor and Emotion*. Cambridge University Press; Kövecses, Z. 2005. *Metaphor in Culture*. Cambridge University Press; Stefanowitsch, A. 2006. Corpus-based approaches to metaphor and metonymy. In A. Stefanowitsch and S. Th. Gries (Eds.), *Corpus-based Approaches to Metaphor and Metonymy* (pp.1–16). Mouton de Gruyter.

194 Forceville, C. 2005. Visual representations of the idealized cognitive model of anger in the Asterix album La Zizanie. *Journal of Pragmatics*, 37: 69–88; Forceville, C. 2011. Pictorial runes in Tintin and the Picaros. *Journal of Pragmatics*, 43: 875–890.

195 McCloud, S. 1993. *Understanding Comics*. Kitchen Sink Press.

196 Díaz-Vera, J. 2013. Woven emotions: Visual representations of emotions in medieval English textiles. *Review of Cognitive Linguistics*, 11/2: 269–284.

197 Source: Adapted from Díaz-Vera 2013, Díaz-Vera, J. 2013. Woven emotions: Visual representations of emotions in medieval English textiles. *Review of Cognitive Linguistics*, 11/2: 269–284.

198 Forceville, C. and E. Urios-Aparisi. 2009. *Multimodal Metaphor*. Mouton de Gruyter; Cohn, N. 2013. *The Visual Language of Comics*. Bloomsbury.

199 Deja, A. 2015. *The Nine Old Men: Lessons, Techniques, and Inspiration from Disney's Great Animators*. Focal Press.

7

200 Source: Emojis provided free by EmojiOne.

201 For an excellent web resource on the history and development of English see: http://www.thehistoryofenglish.com/

202 *Ælfric's Colloquy* (ed. G. N. Garmonsway). 1938. Methuen.

203 Source: Wikimedia Commons.

204 Trudgill, P. 2001. The sociolinguistics of RP. *Sociolinguistic Variation and Change* (chapter 16). Edinburgh University Press.

205 https://www. youtube.com/watch?v=wyRLFWF2v_U.

206 http://www.smithsonianmag.com/smart-news/the-history-of-the-exclamation-point-16445416/?no-ist.

207 The listing of the 2010 emojis are available here: http://emojipedia.org/unicode-6. 0/

208 http://emojipedia.org/grinning-face-with-smiling-eyes/

209 http://grouplens.org/blog/investigating-the-potential-for-miscommunication-using-emoji/

Notes

210 Source: Miller, H., J. Thebault-Spieker, S. Chang, I. Johnson, L. Terveen and B. Hecht. 2016. "Blissfully happy" or "ready to fight": Varying Interpretations of Emoji. *Proceedings of ICWSM 2016*. Menlo Park, CA: AAAI Press. Also in https://grouplens.org/blog/investigating-the-potential-for-miscommunication-using-emoji/

211 Lindstedt, J. 1996. Native Esperanto as a test case for natural language. *SKY Journal of Linguistics*, 19:47–55.

212 Everett, D. 2005. Cultural constraints on grammar and cognition in Pirahã. *Current Anthropology*, 46/4: 621–646.

213 https://www.youtube.com/watch?v=-AgnLH7Dw3w.

214 http://www.plainenglish.co.uk/

215 Corsetti, R. 1996. A mother tongue spoken mainly by fathers. *Language Problems and Language Planning*, 87/4: 63–64.

216 Corsetti, R. 1996. A mother tongue spoken mainly by fathers. *Language Problems and Language Planning*, 20: 3, 263–273.

217 Bergen, B. 2001. Nativization processes in L1 Esperanto. *Journal of Child Language*, 28/3: 575–595.

218 http://mashable.com/2015/06/09/post-hipster-yuccie/#nPtUvj. 0nOq9.

219 Based on a 1973 analysis of the 80,000-word 3rd edition of the *Shorter Oxford Dictionary*.

220 http://www.salon.com/2002/07/22/metrosexual/

221 Based on a 2015 report by Emogi: http://emogi.com/documents/Emoji_Report_2015.pdf.

222 http://www.vogue.com/13372352/jane-fonda-wants-more-feminist-emoji/

223 http://www.theage.com.au/comment/the-fourth-r-missing-from-australian-education-20151025-gkhv8k.html

224 http://www.theguardian.com/commentisfree/2015/jun/21/michael-gove-harry-enfield-grammar-rules-civil-servants.

225 Evans, V. 2015. *The Crucible of Language*. Cambridge University Press.

Epilogue

226 https://www.ted.com/talks/john_underkoffler_drive_3d_data_with_a_gesture?language=en

227 http://www.oblong.com/why-now/hmi/

228 The ratchet effect is a term deriving from economic theory that has been used by psychologist Michael Tomasello to describe the way in which cultural advances lead to an increase in technological and other forms of cultural progress (e.g., Tomasello, M. 1999. *The Cultural Origins of Human Cognition*. Harvard University Press).

229 In 1676, Sir Isaac Newton famously wrote in a letter to Robert Hooke, a fellow scientist and Newton's antagonistic detractor-in-chief: 'If I have seen further it is by standing on the shoulders of giants.'

230 Evans. V. 2015. *The Crucible of Language*. Cambridge University Press.

231 Von Frisch, K. 1953. *The Dancing Bees*. Harvest Books.

232 Zuberbühler, K., D. Jenny and R. Bshary. (1999). The predator deterrence function of primate alarm calls. *Ethology*, 105: 477–490; Fichtel, C., S. Perry and J. Gros-Louis. 2005. Alarm calls of white-faced capuchin monkeys: An acoustic analysis. *Animal Behavior*, 70: 165–176; Ouattara K., A. Lemasson and K. Zuberbühler. 2009. Campbell's monkeys use affixation to alter call meaning. *PLOS ONE* 4/11: e7808.

233 Tomasello, M. 2014. *A Natural History of Human Thinking*. Harvard University Press.

Acknowledgements

Ideas don't come out of thin air. Many people have contributed over the years to my understanding of language and communication – I owe far too many debts of gratitude to single out individuals here. For specific opportunities to work and conduct research in the emerging domain of Emoji as a tool for electronic communication I remain grateful to those companies that have commissioned my research input. These include TalkTalk Mobile, Barclays Bank PLC, O2 Business and Wall's Ice Cream. I have also had outstanding opportunities to publish research on Emoji. I'm grateful, in particular, to the following outlets: *Babel*, Cambridge University Press, *21st Century*, *The Conversation*, the *Guardian*, *Newsweek*, *Lobby*, Oxford University Press and *Psychology Today*. I pay special thanks to my agent, Donald Winchester, for seeing the value in this book, and for his patience, sage counsel and never failing support. I remain grateful to my publishers, Macmillan Picador in the US, and Michael O'Mara Books in the UK for believing in this project, and for my editors Anna DeVries (US) and Fiona Slater (UK). I am especially grateful to Fiona for editing me—the book is so much better than it would otherwise have been for her painstaking work and thoughtful feedback, which led me to explore avenues that I would doubtless not have otherwise wandered down. I also acknowledge all the dedicated Emoji enthusiasts out there, who maintain the range of resources that has made a work such as this possible. In particular, the important work of Jeremy Burge sits in pride of place. Not only did Jeremy found and curate Emojipedia.org, the world's foremost resource site for all things Emoji, but also, among his various other notable achievements, he has given us World Emoji Day. Finally, and above all else, I am eternally grateful to my muse, my wife, Monica.

Photographic Credits

Unless otherwise stated, emojis have been provided free from EmojiOne.

Figure 1 source: Twitter/@andy_murray
Figure 2 source: BBC Newsbeat
Figure 3 source: Twitter/Joe Hale
Figure 4: © ThisisFINLAND.fi
Figure 5 source: WNYC
Figure 6: © Barbara Speed/CityMetric
Figure 7: © Dumpling Emoji Art by Yiying Lu
Figure 8 source: Eggplant Mail
Figure 9: Emojis sourced from (left to right) Microsoft, LG and Apple
Figure 10: Emojis sourced from Apple
Figure 11 source: Twitter/Joe Hale
Figure 12 source: Twitter
Figure 13: © SwiftKey
Figure 14 source: Twitter/@JulieBishopMP
Figure 15: © Joanna Stern/*Wall Street Journal*
Figure 16: Emojis sourced from Apple
Figure 17: © Shigetaka Kurita/Gift of NTT DOCOMO/Museum of Modern Art
Figure 18: © World History Archive / Alamy
Figure 19 source: Miller, H., Thebault-Spieker, J., Chang, S., Johnson, I., Terveen, L., and Hecht, B. (2016) '"Blissfully happy" or "ready to fight": Varying Interpretations of Emoji'. Proceedings of ICWSM 2016. Menlo Park, CA: AAAI Press. Also in https://grouplens.org/blog/investigating-the-potential-for-miscommunication-using-emoji/

Index

Index

Index

Index

Index

Index